QUICK & CLEVER

Christmas Cards

100 FAST & FESTIVE CARDS & TAGS

Elizabeth Moad

D&C
David and Charles

A DAVID & CHARLES BOOK
Copyright © David & Charles Limited 2007

David & Charles is an F+W Publications Inc. company
4700 East Galbraith Road
Cincinnati, OH 45236

First published in the UK in 2007

Text and designs copyright © Elizabeth Moad 2007
Photographs copyright © David & Charles 2007

A catalogue record for this book is available from the British Library.

ISBN-13: 978-0-7153-2592-6 hardback
ISBN-10: 0-7153-2592-2 hardback
ISBN-13: 978-0-7153-2544-5 paperback
ISBN-10: 0-7153-2544-2 paperback

Printed in China
by SNP Leefung
for David & Charles
Brunel House   Newton Abbot   Devon

Executive Editor Cheryl Brown
Desk Editor Bethany Dymond
Senior Designer Tracey Woodward
Design Assistant Eleanor Stafford
Project Editor Jo Richardson
Production Controller Ros Napper
Photography Karl Adamson and Ginette Chapman

Visit our website at www.davidandcharles.co.uk

David & Charles books are available from all good bookshops; alternatively,
you can contact our Orderline on 0870 9908222 or write to us at FREEPOST
EX2 110, D&C Direct, Newton Abbot, TQ12 4ZZ (no stamp required UK only);
US customers call 800-289-0963 and Canadian customers call 800-840-5220.

Christmas Cards

Contents

Introduction

✳ ★ ✳

The giving of Christmas cards is the time-honoured way of sending festive goodwill to loved ones, friends and colleagues. These simple items have the power to strengthen family ties, renew acquaintances and even heal a breach in a personal or business relationship. By spending just a little time and effort on a handmade card, you have the opportunity to make them individual and extra special, and therefore the recipients are sure to appreciate them even more.

Time is always in short supply at Christmas, but handcrafting cards need not be a long, complicated process, yet neither do cards need to be plain and uninteresting to be speedy to create. This book offers a wealth of creative designs for cards that are both quick and clever, including a range of variations and accompanying gift tags for you to make coordinated collections so that everyone receives a unique design. And besides ensuring that you have an extensive resource of design ideas to draw on, there are suggestions for festive greetings and heart-warming sentiments that reflect the design themes, so that you are never lost for words!

Making your own Christmas cards and tags also enables you, as a keen crafter, to put your ever-expanding repertoire of crafting skills to creative use and to showcase those you have developed and honed through the year. Once you realize that family and friends look forward to opening your card in particular, your card crafting will become even more enjoyable and rewarding.

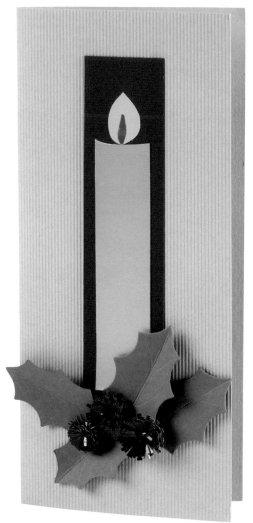

✴ Did You Know? ✴

The Christmas card as we know it today has an interesting history. The custom of sending seasonal messages of goodwill dates back to pagan times, when good-luck charms were exchanged at the winter solstice. In the Victorian era, it was customary for tradesmen to send New Year messages to their clients. But it is Sir Henry Cole who is credited with creating the first commercial Christmas card in the UK, in 1843, and 1,000 copies of the design that he had commissioned, printed and hand-coloured were subsequently sold at one shilling each. However, it took a further 20 years for the concept of the printed Christmas card to become established.

Louis Prang is regarded as the father of the Christmas card in the USA. He began producing cards at his Boston lithograph shop in 1856. Prang's business created much excitement in the art world and succeeded in elevating the status of the greetings card to an art form, since his creations were adorned with silken fringes, cords and tassels – embellishments that are still used now! Given the billions of manufactured and pre-printed Christmas cards that are mailed around the world today, there is all the more reason to make your card stand out from the crowd by creating it yourself, and in the process make your own contribution to the Christmas card's great artistic and social heritage.

★ ✳

How To Use This Book

The book presents 20 wide-ranging design chapters, each one featuring a main 'quick & clever' Christmas card, together with two complementary variations, and a coordinating gift tag, so that you can create a whole themed range of cards for your family and friends. Each lead project itemizes the materials and tools you need, and comes with clear and concise step-by-step instructions and accompanying photographs to help you achieve the best results every time. There are also plenty of practical tips for short cuts and smart solutions.

To help you get started on the projects and support you through the construction and creative processes, the front section includes a quick guide to essential tools and materials, demonstrations of core techniques, advice on more specialized equipment and instructions for making perfect tags, envelopes, boxes and bows.

The express purpose of the Super-Quick Gallery at the end of the book is to help you when the festive frenzy really kicks in and you need some ingenious ideas for cards that can be literally made in minutes.

Making your own cards allows you to give each card a personal significance, and the designs here offer much scope for incorporating names, favourite colours, ages and photographs – including a range of memorable messages and fun greetings – so that projects can be tailored to your intended recipient in one or several ways.

✶ Quick & Clever Card Crafting ✶

✶ **Do** buy enough supplies in one go to avoid multiple shopping trips, and buy pre-folded cards and envelopes in bulk with a friend to save money.

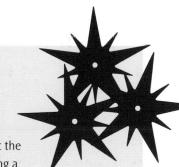

✶ **Do** re-use items from previous years – a rubber stamp from two years ago can be combined with new embellishments.

✶ **Do** try to set aside dedicated time to make cards, to avoid working late at night when your eyes are tired.

✶ **Don't** be over-ambitious about the design you choose when making a batch – consider how long it will take to make each card, and whether the embellishments will be too costly to put on each one or too bulky to mail.

✶ **Don't** try to make all your cards the same. It is much better, especially when you give several cards out in one go, that everyone receives slightly different designs, although simple changes, like the colour theme, are enough.

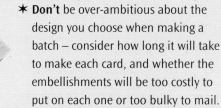

✶ **Don't** panic if you run out of time – the Super-Quick Gallery, pages 100–105, gives you plenty of ways to make great cards from peel-off stickers, toppers and punches with speed!

✶ ✶

Basic Tools

✶ ✶

There are several basic tools that are essential to handcrafting cards, and in the run-up to the busiest time of year, you need tools that you can rely on and those that are the best for the job in hand. Therefore, it is wise to invest in some good-quality items at the outset, from which you will gain maximum benefit.

CUTTING TOOLS

When making a choice, find what you feel most comfortable using. Keep the blades of scissors clean, free of glue residues and also sharp, and replace craft knife blades regularly.

Scissors Choose a large pair for trimming and a small pair for intricate work.

Scoring Tools A special scoring tool can be used for scoring card and paper, but the pointed edge of a bone folder or an empty ballpoint pen can be used instead.

Metal Ruler A metal ruler with a cork base is a good choice, as it is both durable and non-slip.

Paper Trimmers These come in a wide variety, from large to small and from cheap to expensive. They are quick to use and produce a clean, straight cut every time.

Craft Knife and Cutting Mat A craft knife is the best tool for cutting longer straight edges. Always use a craft knife with a metal ruler on a self-healing cutting mat.

ADHESIVES

Different types of adhesive are required for particular purposes, so keep the full range in your kit to achieve the best results.

Clear Adhesive Dots These are available in different sizes and thicknesses. The repositional variety is useful for temporarily adhering an item.

Double-Sided Adhesive Tape Sticky on both sides, this is ideal for mounting work behind apertures.

Adhesive Foam Pads These raise whatever is glued to them away from the surface to give a 3-D effect.

Superglue This powerful glue ensures a long-lasting adhesion of heavier embellishments to cards. Use with extreme care and keep well out of reach of children.

Silicone Adhesive This dries clear and solid, and can be used for tasks where adhesive foam pads may not be suitable.

Spray Glue Useful for sticking larger pieces of card or paper. Use inside an old cardboard box in a well-ventilated area.

Glue Stick This solid glue applies an even coat of adhesive.

PVA (White) Glue This water-based all-purpose glue, which becomes transparent when dry, is suitable for most tasks.

✶ quick & clever ✶

PVA (white) glue makes clearing up quicker, since it is easy to wash off hands and equipment, and it is also the cheapest adhesive.

✶ ✶

Basic Techniques

✶ ✶

A clean cut, score and fold makes a big difference to the final result of a card, so follow these techniques to establish a sound foundation for your card making.

Cutting

quick & clever ✶

Use the grid lines printed on your cutting mat or paper trimmer as guides for cutting to save time measuring.

The quickest and most accurate way to cut paper or card is to use a paper trimmer. Place the paper or card in the paper trimmer and trim to the size required. Alternatively, you can use a craft knife and cutting mat to cut. Measure and mark where you want the cutting line, then place the ruler along the marks and hold firmly in place in one hand while drawing the knife towards you with the other.

Measuring

Use a metal ruler and a sharp HB pencil to mark lightly where you want the cutting line or score line to be at the top and bottom of the paper or card.

quick & clever ✶

If you find that the paper or card becomes shiny with the bone folder, place scrap paper over the fold before creasing with the bone folder.

Scoring

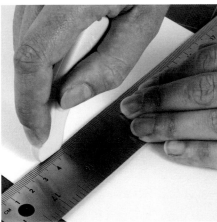

Place the ruler along the pencil marks and hold firmly in place with one hand – a ruler with a cork base is best. With the other hand, draw a scoring tool (see page 8) along the ruler two or three times, pressing firmly down and against the ruler.

Folding

Turn the ruler over so that the cork is uppermost and align with the score line just made. Lift one side of the card up and over the ruler. The ruler edge will assist the fold.

Creasing

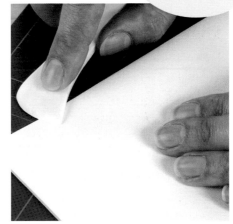

Remove the ruler. Using the flat side of a bone folder, press down firmly all along the folded edge of the card to make a sharp crease.

✶ ✶

Beyond the Basics

★ ★

There are many specialist tools available to crafters, and more being developed all the time. These tools are designed to give a fast and professional result every time, but the more specialist the task they perform, the more expensive the tool is likely to be. Be cautious and build up your tool box over time. In the run-up to Christmas, you may find that you need a specific piece of equipment, so ask family or friends to buy it for you as a gift.

PUNCHES

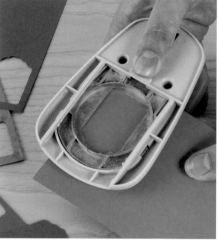

The range of punches available is always increasing. These are a good investment in order to make identical repeat images and can last a long time. If a punch becomes blunt, punch through a piece of kitchen foil to sharpen it.

PUNCH ALIGNERS

A punch aligner allows you to make evenly spaced punches to create borders and other decorations. Although some aligners can only be used with the same brand of punches, they do save time.

DIE-CUTTING TOOLS

★ quick & clever ★

Why not hire a die-cutting tool and templates from a local craft store with a group of fellow crafters and organize a Christmas card-making party?

A large die-cutting tool, such as the one shown here, is a big investment for a crafter, although there are many other types available that are smaller, more portable and less expensive. However, if you are making cards in bulk quantities at Christmas, a die-cutting tool will enable you to make identical shapes quickly and easily, which can then be embellished. The die-cut templates must be purchased separately, but if you have a crafting friend with a compatible machine, you could swap templates to give you a wider range of shapes to use.

EYELETS

These are metal embellishments used to attach panels to cards, to thread cord through or for purely decorative purposes. The range of eyelets is increasing, so look out in craft shops for new varieties especially designed with Christmas in mind.

Most eyelets require a punch, setting tool and hammer to punch a hole, flatten the eyelet and secure in place, but no-set eyelets are available that do not require these tools, so are extra quick to use.

★ ★

RUBBER STAMPS

These come in a wide range of festive designs to meet all tastes, from cute hedgehogs, Santas and robins to more traditional floral motifs. They can be used to create background designs or borders for cards and tags, as well as to decorate envelopes or boxes for packaging cards. Take care of your stamps at this busy time when they are used over and over again by ensuring that they are thoroughly cleaned after each project, and don't throw them into a drawer to be sorted out after Christmas, as the rubber image can easily be damaged.

★ quick & clever ★

If you are using a specialist inkpad such as StazOn™, make sure you buy the appropriate cleaning product at the same time.

SHAPE TEMPLATES AND CUTTING TOOLS

Plastic templates of various shapes and sizes can be used in conjunction with a cutting tool to cut apertures, trim images or make tags (see page 15), and enable difficult shapes to be cut with speed and accuracy. Always use on a cutting mat.

EMBOSSING SYSTEMS

There are various embossing systems available that do not require a lightbox, making them quick and easy to use. Paper, lightweight card and parchment paper can be embossed (see Simply Snow, pages 28–31).

RUBBER STAMPING TECHNIQUES

There are many techniques in rubber stamping, but the two demonstrated here are especially quick and clever when making Christmas cards.

Fading Out

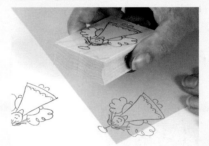

Ink your stamp as usual, but print onto scrap paper first, then print onto the main card. This produces a lighter effect, which is ideal for creating backgrounds.

Tapestry

Ink one stamp and print at full strength onto the card so that it stands out – in this case, the gingerbread man – and around which the other prints will go. Ink another stamp, in this case a leaf, and print at full strength between the first design, then print again without re-inking. Build up the tapestry effect by continuing this combination of darker and lighter prints (see Home Sweet Home, page 24).

Festive Supplies

* *

There are a few who are immune to the magic of Christmas, but no crafter can resist those tempting papers, ribbons, brads, eyelets, peel-off stickers and toppers in all their glorious colours, shapes and sizes. While the festive season is a great opportunity to indulge in some new items, you may be surprised to discover most of what you need already on your shelves, so check your stores before you go shopping.

PAPERS

There are many varieties of printed paper and card available. The card stock and pads of papers designed for scrapbooking can be used for card making, and booklets of printed images offer a creative resource (see Stocking Surprise, page 84).

PEEL-OFF STICKERS

These provide an almost endless range of ready-to-use designs and motifs, available in a variety of different forms, such as outline, solid, embossed, 3-D and resin.

LASER-CUTS

These are very intricate shapes that have been cut by a laser. They come in sheets of different shapes or designs.

3-D PAINT

This very thick liquid paint, applied directly from the tube, comes in many colours and can be used on most surfaces to give dimension and texture. It dries quickly in small quantities, but more liberal application requires overnight drying.

RUB-ON TRANSFERS

Flatter than peel-off stickers, these adhesive images need to be transferred to paper or card by rubbing with the back of a teaspoon.

RIBBONS

Ribbons are a great way of adding a festive touch to a card. Readily available from haberdashery shops, craft stores and suppliers also stock a wide range of printed ribbons. A bow also jazzes up a tag, envelope or box, which can be coordinated with the card.

BRADS

Also known as paper fasteners and originally a standard stationery item in their round form, brads now come in squares, snowflakes, trees, hearts and many more designs.

QUILLING PAPERS

Gold-, silver- and copper-edged quilling papers are available and are fantastic for festive quilling.

TOPPERS

This is the term used for ready-made embellishments, which come in a wide array of sizes, shapes, colours and designs.

Health and Safety

★ Remember that embellishments are not suitable for young children, as they are a choking hazard.

★ Some embellishments, such as brads and eyelets, may have sharp edges on the reverse, which should be covered over, especially if mailing.

* *

TYING A BOW

Bows play a leading role in festive designs, so it makes sense to take a little time to perfect your bow-tying technique. Most people learn to tie a shoestring bow as a child, but these two other bows offer a more professional finish.

Double-Loop Bow

1 With the ribbon still on the roll or the length untrimmed, form a loop towards the cut end of the ribbon and hold with one hand.

2 Make a second loop of the same size a little further along the ribbon, away from the cut end, and hold in your other hand.

3 Take one loop and pass it over the top of the other loop.

4 Pass this loop over and back through between the two loops.

5 Pull the loops tight (if your ribbon has a right and reverse side, like this velvet example, you may need to twist it to turn the right side uppermost). The loops may be longer than desired, so pull the ends of the ribbon to shorten the loops.

6 Cut the bow from the roll or length of ribbon and trim the ends into a 'V' shape.

Multi-Loop Bow

1 With the ribbon still on the roll or the length untrimmed, make four loops, with the top loops slightly smaller.

2 Cut the loops from the roll or length of ribbon and pinch the centres of the loops together between your fingers.

3 Take a 10cm (4in) length of thin wire (gauge 34) and wrap it tightly around the centre of the bow several times. Twist the ends of the wire together and trim with scissors or pliers.

4 Take a length of the same ribbon and tie in a knot around the centre of the bow.

5 Pull the ends of the ribbon tight to cover the wire around the loops.

✳ ✳

Making Tags

★ ★

When making a card, it is easy to make a coordinated tag for an accompanying gift at the same time, and there are many quick and clever ways in which to create tags, as demonstrated here.

DIE-CUTS

Place the die-cut template on the base plastic sheet, then place the card on top, ensuring that the entire template is covered. Place the second plastic sheet on top, then place all four layers in the die-cutter. Turn the handle to draw the 'sandwich' through. Once on the other side, remove the top layer to reveal the tags.

RUBBER STAMPS

These are a quick way of making unusual tags. They can be printed with a standard inkpad or you could take the creative process further and use heat embossing.

PUNCHES

Use these to cut out tags from card in moments, with many different sizes to choose from, the mini ones being ideal for making tags to embellish cards.

This tag stamp had two elements to its design, which were highlighted with two different colours of brush marker applied directly to the stamp – brush markers allow you to colour in specific areas. The stamp was printed onto blue card, then cut out with scissors, a hole punched in the top and silver cord threaded through.

For this tag, the tag stamp was simply inked and printed onto blue card. It was then cut out with scissors and a hole punched in the top with a mini holepunch.

READY-MADE TAGS

Crafters have been cleverly using luggage tags, available from stationery shops and suppliers, in their card making, scrapbooking and other crafting pursuits for years. The tags come in many different sizes and are a super-quick alternative to cutting your own.

SHAPE CUTTERS

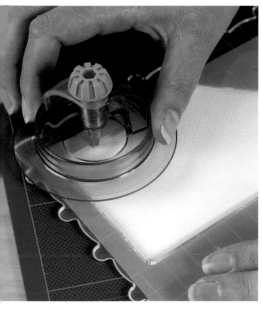

Place the card on a cutting mat. Put a plastic tag template on top and hold in place with one hand. Position the cutting tool inside the tag shape with the swivel blade at the edge. Drag the tool around the template to cut the shape.

SEWING MACHINE

A sewing machine is a quick and easy way to decorate a tag (or card). Here, one tag was cut using a template and then a slightly larger version cut, and the two stitched together with a zigzag stitch.

★ quick & clever ★

Look out for portable mini sewing machines designed for crafting, but they may only offer one stitch type.

Plastic Tag Templates

Plastic templates offer tags in many different shapes and sizes to choose from.

step one Place your chosen template on the card. Use a sharp HB pencil to draw through the template onto the card. To save both paper and time, you can line the template up with a straight edge of the card, to avoid having to cut one of the tag sides. Remove the template and cut out the shape with scissors.

step two Use a holepunch to punch a hole in the top of the tag for threading. Here, the punch is held upside down and the tag slotted into the punch so that the pencil mark made from the template is visible through the punch, to allow correct positioning. Use an eraser to rub out any pencil marks left on the tag.

✱ ✱

Sending Your Cards

✱ ✱ ✱ ✱ ✱ ✱ ✱ ✱ ✱ ✱ ✱ ✱ ✱ ✱ ✱ ✱ ✱ ✱

The presentation of your cards is important and extends to the way in which they are packaged. A specially crafted envelope or box provides the perfect finishing touch, and also protects the handmade item within to ensure that it is received in optimum condition.

MAKING ENVELOPES

The quickest and easiest way to make an envelope is to use a plastic envelope template (see below). Use a strong paper or lightweight card that is easily folded. Heavy card will be too stiff to fold crisply and will add to the cost of mailing.

Many printed papers are strong enough to make envelopes, such as those shown above, which can be chosen to coordinate with the card inside.

Using a Plastic Envelope Template

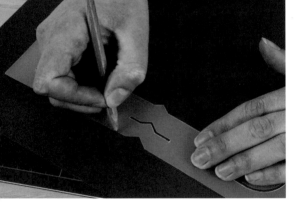

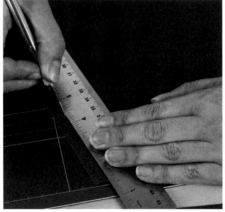

step one Place the paper or card on a cutting mat, then place the template on top. Draw around the template with a sharp HB pencil. This one has three sizes – here, the outer, largest size was chosen.

step two Place a metal ruler along the pencil lines just drawn and cut with a craft knife. Scissors can be used instead. Using a scoring tool (see page 8) and the metal ruler, score along all four flaps.

step three Use the ruler to make a sharp fold, then press the crease with the flat side of a bone folder (see page 9). Glue the bottom flap over the two side flaps, then glue the top flap down once the card is inside.

USING READY-MADE ENVELOPES

If you don't have enough time to make a special envelope, you can easily jazz up a ready-made envelope to coordinate with the card inside. Here, the pink envelope was rubber-stamped, the green has three tree punches attached, the red has gold rub-on stars and the blue has white peel-off stickers.

✱ ✱

Boxes

Making a small box for your card takes only a short time, and for those few extra minutes spent, not only will the card be well protected, but the recipient will be impressed by the tailor-made packaging – especially if it is decorated. Always use card to make boxes for greetings cards.

When making a box for a card, a professional result is achieved if a coordinating colour is used, as in this example, where the box encases a quilled candle card (see A Christmas Carol, page 72).

step one Enlarge the template on page 106 on a photocopier. Cut along the outside solid lines, then draw around the template onto scrap card and cut out using a craft knife and metal ruler. Draw around onto card and cut out.

step two Place the box, right side down, on a cutting mat. Using a scoring tool (see page 8) and a metal ruler, score along all the dashed lines marked on the template on page 106. Fold and crease along the score lines (see page 9).

step three To decorate the box, turn it over so that the right side is uppermost. Here, a simple holly rubber stamp is printed in each of the four corners of what will become the box lid.

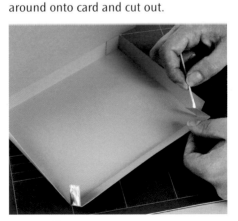

step four Apply PVA (white) glue with a cocktail stick to each of the four tabs on the base of the box. Press these tabs to the inside of the box side to complete the box base. The lid will then fit neatly into the box base. A coordinating ribbon can be wrapped around the box and tied in a bow to finish.

Postwise

★ Keep any decoration to the left-hand side of the envelope so that it does not detract from the address.

★ Use a white sticky label on dark envelopes on which to write the address, so that it is clearly legible.

★ Reserve the use of trinkets and any bulky embellishments for the card inside only.

★ If the card has any delicate elements or embellishments that may poke through the envelope during transit in the mail, cover it with a piece of bubble wrap for protection.

FAST & FESTIVE CARDS & TAGS

Perfect Presents

A card that resembles a gift is guaranteed to grab attention! This is easily achieved using the template provided to make the base card, and professional ribbon-tying adds the perfect finishing touch.

A bold gift shape is cut from red card in the main project, and punched circles are used to create a giftwrap-style design. A gold ribbon is tied round and through the card spine, ending in a flamboyant bow at the top. A simple change of card shape creates an alternative gift-box design, but if time is really short, the other variation shows how to give a pre-cut square card the gift-effect treatment.

✴ Prettily Packaged ✴

A wide strip of the same coloured card was cut to make a lid for an orange single-fold card. Before it was glued in place, a simple pattern was added to the main card, with diagonal lines drawn in orange marker pen, then drawn across again with an orange glaze pen. The same pen was then used to add a border to the lid. Bright pink ribbon, tied in a double-loop bow at the top (see page 13), completes the look.

✴ It's a Wrap ✴

This super-quick variation on the gift theme uses a gold standard square single-fold card. The card was decorated all over with bright pink punched stars to resemble giftwrap. A length of pink striped ribbon was then tied package-style around the card, finishing with a double-loop bow at the centre (see page 13). The ends of the ribbon were then secured in place with small pieces of double-sided adhesive tape.

Perfect Presents

You will need

* red card 20 x 30cm (8 x 12in)
* pink and orange card 10cm (4in) square
* 1m (1yd) length of gold ribbon
* circle punches – 1.5cm (⅝in), 1cm (⅜in)
* Basic Tool Kit (see page 8)

step one Enlarge the template on page 106 on a photocopier and cut out. Draw around onto the wrong side of the red card with a sharp HB pencil and cut out with a craft knife and metal ruler on a cutting mat (if making more than one card, draw around onto scrap card and cut out to make your own template).

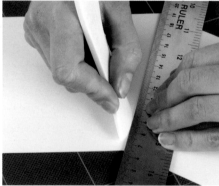

step two Place the ruler to align with the two inner corners of the card and score across the card with a scoring tool (see page 8).

quick & clever

Don't forget to coordinate the envelope for the card with a matching bow.

step three
Turn the card over so that the red side is uppermost on the cutting mat. Use the craft knife to cut a slit in the centre of the spine to accommodate the particular width of ribbon you are using. In this case, 1.5cm (⅝in) wide ribbon was used.

step four Punch 11 x 1.5cm (⅝in) circles from pink card and 11 x 1cm (⅜in) circles from orange card.

step five

Using PVA (white) glue, stick the larger pink circles all over the front panel of the card, then glue the smaller orange circles on top, slightly off-centre to the pink.

step six

Thread the ribbon through the slit in the spine of the card and pull through to halfway along the length of the ribbon.

A gift of good wishes for you this Christmas

step seven

Turn the card over and twist the two lengths of ribbon together, then take one over the top of the card and one over the bottom. The twisted ribbon will squash flat, or stick it down on the reverse side with double-sided adhesive tape.

step eight

Take the two ends of the ribbon and tie in a double-loop bow (see page 13) at the top of the card. Trim the ends of the ribbon diagonally.

Tag it!

A mini gift card makes a fun tag. Here, a small gold single-fold card was decorated with two shades of orange punched circles in two different sizes. A length of red and slightly narrower orange ribbon were tied one on top of the other around the tag, finishing in a double-loop bow (see page 13) at the top as in the main card.

✱ quick & clever ✱

You could use sticky-backed ribbon instead of ordinary ribbon and tie a separate bow at the top of the card.

Jolly Gingerbread Man

A shaped card will really stand out from the crowd, and this charming gingerbread man example is very quick to make by folding card in half and cutting out the front and back, using the template supplied, in one go.

The warm brown card is sponged around the edges with a darker brown ink for a rounded, toasted effect, and the front decorated with white 3-D paint, pens and a bright red bow to bring him to life. You could tuck an invitation to a festive meal or a children's party inside the card. The gingerbread theme is continued in the variations, but featuring toppers and rubber stamps for those who find cutting shapes daunting.

✳ Home Sweet Home ✳

The rubber stamping tapestry technique (see page 11) was used to create a gingerbread man border on a cream card, with the eyes and buttons coloured in with black pen. A felt topper of a gingerbread house was attached to a square of copper card, then embellished with a border of white 3-D paint, applied as a row of dots to resemble icing, and also to avoid the effort of attempting to achieve straight lines.

✳ Gingerbread Gang ✳

The gingerbread men are wooden toppers that came complete with white markings, but these were enhanced by applying a layer of white 3-D paint on top for an icing-type effect. They were then mounted onto rectangles of cream card. Copper-coloured organza ribbon was tied around the centre of a matching landscape-shaped single-fold card, with the fold at the top, and a knot tied at each end. The cream panels were then stuck in a row over the ribbon with double-sided adhesive tape and a dot of white 3-D paint added to each corner to finish.

Jolly Gingerbread Man

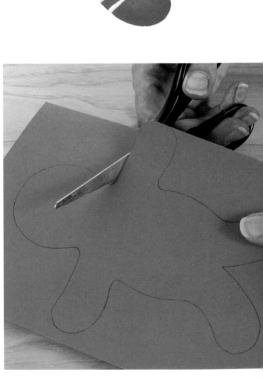

You will need

* brown card A4 (US letter)
* brown inkpad
* black pen or 2 small black buttons
* white 3-D paint
* 30cm (12in) length of narrow red ribbon
* small piece of clean sponge or sponge dauber
* sewing needle and black sewing thread (optional)
* Basic Tool Kit (see page 8)

step one Use a metal ruler and a sharp HB pencil to lightly mark the halfway point along each long edge of the brown card. Place the ruler along the pencil marks, score along the ruler and fold the card in half. Use the flat side of a bone folder to make a sharp crease.

★ quick & clever ★

Instead of using the template provided, you could simply draw around a gingerbread man cookie cutter if you have one.

step two Photocopy the gingerbread man template on page 108 onto paper and cut out. Draw around onto one side of the folded brown card with the pencil (if making more than one card, draw around onto scrap card and cut out to make your own template). Make sure that the end of one arm butts up to the fold, as this needs to remain uncut.

step three Use a medium-sized pair of scissors to cut out the shape, cutting through both pieces of the card in one go. Do not cut through the arm on the fold, as this is needed to keep the gingerbread men joined together.

Use a black glaze pen for adding the eyes, as here, if you want to make them shiny, otherwise any black pen is suitable.

step four Keep the shaped card folded and place on scrap paper. Press the piece of sponge or sponge dauber into a brown inkpad to pick up ink. Gently dab all around the edges of the gingerbread man with the sponge or dauber, transferring the ink to the card. Discard the scrap paper to avoid transferring unwanted ink elsewhere.

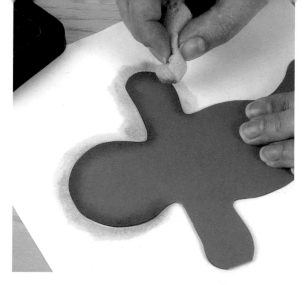

'Tis the season to be jolly

* quick & clever *

To speed up the drying of the 3-D paint, place near a radiator or other heat source, taking care of fire hazards. Or use a thick white marker pen instead.

Tag it!

For a coordinating tag, two tag shapes of the same size, one red, one striped, were cut using a plastic tag template and glued together. A hole was punched in the top with a mini holepunch. The corners of a smaller piece of red card were rounded using a corner punch and glued to the striped side of the tag. A gingerbread man peel-off sticker was then attached to the red panel, with two candy cane stickers either side. Green ribbon was tied through the tag to finish.

step five Add eyes to the gingerbread man with a black pen. Alternatively, sew or superglue on buttons for eyes. Place the folded shaped card on a clean piece of scrap paper. Take a tube of white 3-D paint and squirt a little onto scrap paper to get the paint flowing and to gauge how hard you need to squeeze. Use to decorate the gingerbread man as shown in the main card photo. Leave to dry according to the manufacturer's instructions.

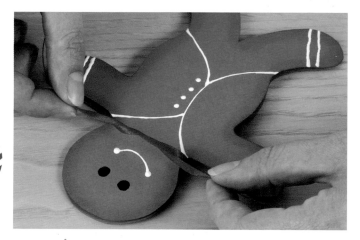

step six Tie the length of ribbon in a shoestring or double-loop bow (see page 13) around the gingerbread man's neck. Trim the ends of the ribbon diagonally.

Simply Snow

Christmas means glitter and lots of it! And here it adds its magical sparkle to the art of embossing on translucent parchment paper, which results in a design highlighted in slight relief and a subtle change of tone.

The main card features a snowflake-patterned background embossed onto the parchment paper using an embossing system and template, secured to the base card with novelty snowflake-shaped eyelets. A punched snowflake, framed within a blue glitter circle, provides the focal point. The two variations illustrate how contrasting yet still very contemporary effects can be created from applying the same three elements of parchment paper, glitter and punches in different ways.

✳ Winter Tapestry ✳

A row of snowflakes was punched out around each edge of a parchment paper square using a punch aligner to aid positioning (see page 10), then a snowflake punched from double-sided adhesive paper and attached to the centre. The top layer of the central snowflake was removed and the snowflake sprinkled with blue ultra-fine glitter. The parchment paper panel was then mounted onto a blue single-fold card using pale blue corner brads.

✳ Snow Drops ✳

A strip of large spotted printed paper was used to create the left-hand border of this dark blue single-fold card, which was then enhanced with snowflakes punched from double-sided adhesive paper, the top layer removed and sprinkled with purple ultra-fine glitter. A circle punch was used to make an aperture in the top right-hand section of the single-fold card, and a piece of parchment paper embossed with a snowflake mounted behind.

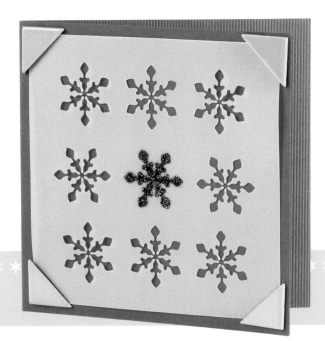

Simply Snow

You will need

- ✳ sheet of double-sided adhesive paper
- ✳ parchment paper 20 x 13cm (8 x 5in)
- ✳ sheet of white paper
- ✳ blue single-fold card 17.5 x 8cm (6⅞ x 3⅛in)
- ✳ blue ultra-fine glitter
- ✳ snowflake-shaped eyelets
- ✳ punches – 5cm (2in) circle, snowflake
- ✳ medium ball embossing tool
- ✳ Fiskars® ShapeBoss™ and 'Winter Wonderland' embossing stencil
- ✳ old cutting mat
- ✳ eyelet punch, setting tool and hammer
- ✳ Basic Tool Kit (see page 8)

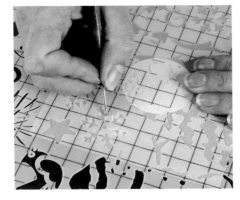

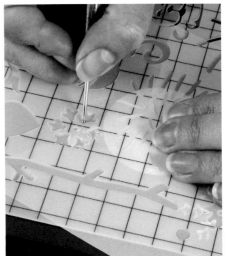

step one Punch a circle from double-sided adhesive paper. Remove the backing paper and position the circle towards the top of the parchment paper. Do not remove the top layer of the paper at this stage.

step two Lift the top plastic stencil sheet of the embossing system and insert the parchment paper. Ensure that the side with the punched circle is face down. Position under a snowflake. Using a medium ball embossing tool, emboss the outline.

✳ quick & clever ✳

You may find that rubbing the parchment paper with an anti-static bag before step four helps to prevent glitter from clinging to any unwanted areas.

step three Move the parchment paper around in the template and emboss another snowflake. Continue embossing until the area around the circle is covered with snowflakes.

step four Using a metal ruler and craft knife on a cutting mat, trim the parchment paper to 16 x 7.5cm (6¼ x 3in). You will find that the edges of some snowflakes are trimmed off, but this adds to the effect. Punch a snowflake from white paper. Remove the top layer from the punched circle of adhesive paper.

step five

Place the white snowflake in the centre of the adhesive circle. Put the parchment paper on a piece of scrap paper and sprinkle generous amounts of blue ultra-fine glitter over the sticky area.

step six

Shake off the excess glitter onto the scrap paper and return the spare glitter to its container. If there is glitter on the white snowflake, use a clean, dry fine paintbrush to remove it.

White Christmas wishes

step seven

Place the opened-out single-fold card, right side up, on an old cutting mat with the parchment paper on the right-hand side. Make a hole in each corner with the eyelet punch and hammer.

step eight

Holding the parchment paper in place, insert an eyelet into each hole, with the snowflake on the 'good' side of the card. Use the setting tool and hammer to fix each eyelet in place.

Tag it!

For this glittering tag, four snowflakes were punched from double-sided adhesive paper. The backing sheet was removed from each and they were placed on a pale blue tag, with some protruding over the edge, which were then trimmed to align with the edge. The top layer was removed from each snowflake, then dark blue ultra-fine glitter shaken all over the shapes and the excess shaken off. A hole was punched in the top with a mini holepunch, then pale blue ribbon threaded through and tied in a bow.

Dreaming of a white Christmas

Sparkling Stars

Bring an extra sparkle to the festive scene with the clever use of sequins. By threading star-shaped sequins onto metallic thread and allowing them to hang, they create a dazzling display as they turn and twinkle.

In the main card, silver threads of sequins cascade over a central silver and green star, mounted on a funky background of bright pink felt punctuated by silver card strips. The accompanying designs explore further the creative combination of sequins and felt, using both extra-large and different-coloured small star sequins, to complete a range of cards that will have strong appeal to teenage girls.

✳ Starbursts ✳

A silver single-fold card pre-cut with a row of three square apertures was used for this variation on the star theme, and a rectangle of bright pink felt placed on the reverse of the front panel of the card with double-sided adhesive tape. A large star sequin was then sewn to each square of pink felt using silver metallic thread, with a pink bead added to the centre of each light-catching star.

✳ Falling Stars ✳

Different-coloured star sequins were threaded onto three silver strands, which were then attached to a strip of pink card. This was mounted onto a tall silver single-fold card. White felt was glued to a card square and attached over the strands of sequins. A silver star outline peel-off sticker was placed onto pink card and cut out, and repeated with a smaller silver star and paler pink card. The two stars were then glued together and attached to the white felt.

Sparkling Stars

quick & clever

If you are short of time, place silver star solid peel-off stickers directly onto the pink felt instead of threading the star sequins.

step one Rub a glue stick all over the front panel of the green single-fold card, leaving a 1cm (⅜in) margin around the edges. Place the square of pink felt centrally on the front of the card and press down.

step two Place the silver card on a cutting mat. Using a metal ruler and craft knife, cut five strips, angling the cuts so that the strips are narrower at one end.

step three Attach the silver card strips to the pink felt with PVA (white) glue, positioning them evenly spaced across the felt and with the points facing in alternate directions.

step four Thread a 30cm (12in) length of silver metallic thread onto a sewing needle. Thread the needle and thread through a silver star sequin, then tie a knot in the thread.

step five Thread another star sequin onto the thread and leave about a 2cm (¾in) gap between the star sequins, then tie a knot. Tie three more star sequins onto the thread in the same way. Repeat with another 30cm (12in) length of silver thread, but thread on four star sequins, then with another length, but thread on five star sequins, and with a final length, but thread on four star sequins.

step six Open the card out and place on a foam pad. Insert the needle threaded with one sequin thread through the top of the felt and card midway between the first two silver strips. Pull through to the first star.

Christmas wishes on a star

step seven Remove the needle and secure the thread on the reverse side with a silver star peel-off sticker. Trim the excess thread from this side and the end threaded with sequins so that it falls level with the bottom edge of the pink felt. Repeat with the remaining sequin threads.

step eight Photocopy the two star templates on page 109 onto paper and cut out. Draw around the larger star onto green card and the smaller one onto silver card with a sharp HB pencil and cut out. Carefully lay the sequin threads above the card and attach the card star centrally to the pink felt panel, over the silver strips. Lay the sequin threads back down so that they hang in front of the central star.

Tag it!

To create this dynamic star tag, a pink felt star was glued to a slightly larger, pale pink card star. A silver star solid peel-off sticker was then positioned in the centre of the pink felt star. A hole was punched with a mini holepunch through the tip of one point of the pink card star, then white narrow organza ribbon threaded through and tied in a knot.

✳ quick & clever ✳

If you don't have any pink felt to hand, you can use bright pink card instead.

Starry Night

Rubber stamping is an ideal way of creating Christmas cards because it allows identical repeat images to be created quickly. Stamps also enable you to achieve a professional look but retain a handmade feel. Make your stamps work hard for you at this busy time by investing in a coordinated set.

Here, a trio of stamps has been used to create a unique range of cards on the same fun theme. In the main project, one hedgehog stamp is inked and printed, then coloured in using diluted felt-tip pen and a fine paintbrush for a soft, watercolour effect. The variation cards are similarly made using the other two stamps in this festive set. By experimenting with different colours and colouring-in mediums, such as real watercolour inks and colouring pencils, you can produce yet more variations from one stamp set.

✳ Prickly Kisses ✳

The second hedgehog stamp was printed onto white card and coloured in. The stamped card was then mounted onto turquoise card with adhesive foam pads, which in turn was glued to a pearlescent blue square single-fold card. Three star-shaped sequins were threaded onto blue cotton, tied in place at evenly spaced intervals and attached to the bottom of the card (see pages 34–35).

✳ Baubling Along ✳

The third hedgehog stamp was stamped and coloured in. One bauble at a time was dampened with a paintbrush and then colour applied directly with a felt-tip pen. A craft knife was used to cut around the baubles and hedgehogs, and the stamped panel mounted onto dark blue card, then in turn onto a purple single-fold card with the fold at the top. Gold star peel-off stickers decorate the blue card for a starry night effect.

Starry Night

You will need

* white card 12 x 21cm (4¾ x 8¼in)
* blue single-fold card 10.5 x 15cm (4¼ x 6in), fold at the top
* hedgehog rubber stamp
* black StazOn™ inkpad and StazOn™ cleaner
* felt-tip pens: pink, grey, blue
* fine gold marker pen (or silver, yellow or any other colour)
* gold rub-on stars
* Basic Tool Kit (see page 8)

quick & clever ✶

Be sure to use a plain white saucer or small plate with this watercolour technique, since any pattern will distract you from the colour mixing and diluting.

step one Ink the whole hedgehog rubber stamp with the black StazOn™ inkpad. Place the white card on a clean, flat surface and press down with the stamp firmly. Lift the stamp off the card directly to avoid smudging.

step two Rub a pink felt-tip pen onto a clean, white saucer or small plate to leave a residue of pink ink.

step three Dip a fine paintbrush into a jar of clean water and mix with the ink on the saucer or plate. Do this two or three times and then test the colour on scrap white card. If it is too pink, continue to dilute with water until it is a light pink colour.

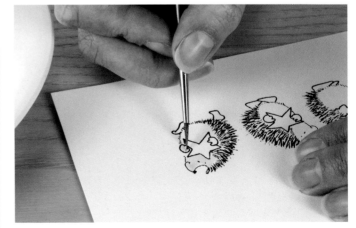

step four Wash the paintbrush in the water and dab onto clean kitchen paper. Pick up a little diluted pink ink with the tip of the paintbrush and colour in the faces, hands and feet of the hedgehogs. Take care not to go over the edges.

step five Rinse the brush well in the jar of water. Rub grey felt-tip pen onto another area of the saucer or plate and dilute as in step three. Pick up a little diluted grey ink with the paintbrush and colour in the hedgehogs' bodies. Use the same diluted grey ink to mark in an arm reaching for the star on the second from left hedgehog with a few strokes of the paintbrush. Colour in the ground a light grey and the background light blue.

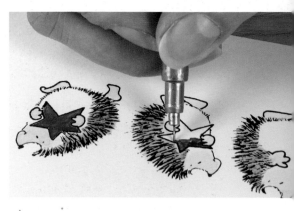

step six Colour in the star shapes with a fine gold marker pen. Alternatively, use silver, yellow or any colour you wish.

step seven Place the stamped white card on a cutting mat and use a craft knife to cut around the tops of the hedgehogs in a single curved motion. Trim the ends so that the card measures 15cm (6in) in length.

step eight Attach the hedgehog panel to the blue single-fold card with PVA (white) glue. Cut around a gold rub-on star and remove the backing paper. Position the star on the blue card and use the back of a teaspoon to rub over the star firmly. Remove the clear plastic, leaving the star in place. Repeat with different-sized stars all over the card.

Tag it!

To create a coordinating tag, just two hedgehogs were inked on the main stamp with the black StazOn™ inkpad and printed onto a square of white card. The hedgehogs' faces, background and stars were coloured in as for the main card, but using brown felt-tip pen for the hedgehogs' bodies. The stamped white card was mounted onto a gold square single-fold card. A hole was punched through the back panel with a regular office holepunch, then a length of gold ribbon threaded through and tied in a knot.

Have a jolly holiday

quick & clever

Card will vary in absorbency between manufacturers, so test out the watercolour technique first on a scrap of your chosen card to check that you are happy with it.

Trim the Trees

Stitching with a sewing machine is an incredibly easy way to create a unique card. A simple zigzag stitch in a bright sewing thread makes a bold statement and adds textural interest, while performing the function of holding layers of card together.

In the main design, strips of bright red card are machine stitched onto white linen-effect card to create a stylish, stylized tree image. The thread ends are neatly tidied away on the reverse side, which is then topped with a punched star. The variation cards use the same zigzag stitch to add patterned bands around a traditional bauble shape and vertically to enhance a trio of candles.

✳ Hanging Treasure ✳

Two lines of dark green zigzag stitches were machine stitched across a light green card bauble (template A on page 107). Pinking shears were used to cut a strip of darker green card for a central decorative band and silver card for the bauble top. A small wire loop was attached to the bauble top and a green multi-loop ribbon bow (see page 13) tied through. The bauble was mounted onto green card with adhesive foam pads and then onto a lighter green single-fold card.

✳ Candle Centrepiece ✳

Three strips of white textured card were glued vertically to gold card and then machine stitched down the centre with a line of red zigzag stitches. The thread ends were pulled through to the reverse side as in the main card and the gold card attached to a red single-fold card. Flame shapes were cut from yellow card and glued to the tops of the candles. Finally, orange felt-tip pen was used to add a touch of colour to the centre of each flame.

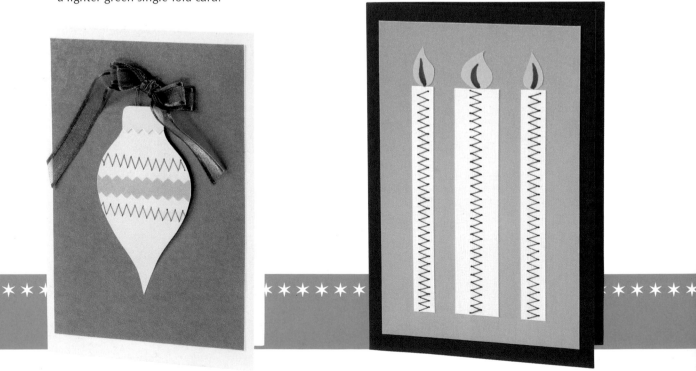

Trim the Trees

*Tree Cheers
for Christmas
and New Year's*

step one

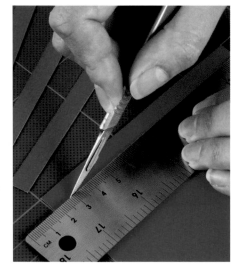

Place the red card on a cutting mat. Using a metal ruler and a craft knife, cut strips 1cm (⅜in) wide and 13cm (5in) long. You may wish to use a paper trimmer for extra speed.

step two

Cut the strips into five lengths of 9.5cm, 8cm, 6cm, 4cm and 2.5cm (3¾in, 3⅛in, 2⅜in, 1½in and 1in) and place, right side down, on scrap paper. Use a glue stick to attach each piece to the white card square as shown in the main card photo.

quick & clever

Use card that is only shiny on one side, otherwise the sewing machine foot will slip and your stitching will be irregular. Use large, widely spaced stitches for best results.

step three

Set your sewing machine to zigzag stitch and sew along the centre of the longest strip. Remove the card from the machine and trim either end of the thread to 10cm (4in) in length. Repeat with the remaining strips. If you haven't used your machine with card before, test first on scrap card.

step four

Starting with the bottom strip on the right side, thread the end of the sewing thread onto the needle. Take the needle through to the reverse side of the card, pulling the thread all the way through, then remove the thread from the needle. Repeat for either end of each strip.

step five

Turn the card over so that the right side is face down and place two lengths of adhesive tape over the thread ends to make sure that they don't unravel. Trim the excess thread with scissors.

Enjoy your tree time

step six Place double-sided adhesive tape along each edge on the reserve of the white card. Peel off the backing of each tape piece halfway and fold outwards. Position the card, right side up, over the red single-fold card, then remove all the tape backing.

quick & clever ✶

If you don't have a sewing machine, use a fine pen to draw on a stitched effect (see Rudolph the Reindeer, pages 52–55), or rubber stamps are available that will print a zigzag line to resemble stitching.

step seven Punch a star and cut a tree base 1.3 x 1cm (½ x ⅜in) from red card, then glue both in place on the white card.

Tag it!

A matching tag was made by cutting a simple tree shape from white card and then machine sewing to a red card triangle with red running stitch. The thread ends were taken through to the reverse side as in the main card and a second card triangle glued to the reverse side to cover the stitching and allow for a message to be written. A hole was punched in the top with a mini holepunch, then red organza ribbon threaded through and tied in a bow.

Pretty Poinsettias

Rubber stamp heat embossing is a quicker and easier technique than may first appear. The motif is printed, sprinkled with embossing powder and then heated to create a raised image. This then provides a framework for adding colour.

Here, the poinsettia flower is celebrated, its bright red flowers perfectly in keeping with the traditional festive colours. White embossing powder is heated to give a delicate outline, within which the flowers and leaves are coloured. Inkpads provide the strong vibrant colours, which are applied with a paintbrush. The variation cards use gold and silver embossing powder, illustrating that all three colours work equally well.

✳ Gorgeously Gilded ✳

This trio of images was taken from a single rubber stamp. The stamp was inked and printed onto pale green card, then gold embossing powder applied and heated. The images were coloured in using the same technique as for the main card. Each square was carefully cut around and mounted onto torn dark green paper to set off the gold, which in turn was mounted onto a gold single-fold card.

✳ Flowery Gates ✳

This unusually shaped stamp was printed twice onto white cartridge paper. Silver embossing powder was applied and heated, as in the main card. Both designs were coloured in and carefully cut out, then one mounted onto each front panel of a green gatefold card. A small hole was punched halfway down the outside edge of each front panel with a mini holepunch, then narrow ribbon threaded through and tied in a shoestring bow to close.

Pretty Poinsettias

You will need

* 140lb (300g/m²) watercolour paper or strong cartridge paper
* green card 13.5 x 9.5cm (5¼ x 3¾in)
* red single-fold card 15 x 10.5cm (6 x 4⅛in)
* poinsettia rubber stamp
* inkpads – clear embossing, red, green, brown
* white embossing powder
* yellow glaze pen
* 1cm (⅜in) wide dark-edged green organza ribbon
* anti-static bag
* tile or other heatproof surface
* wooden clothes peg
* heat gun
* Basic Tool Kit (see page 8)

step one Rub the watercolour or cartridge paper all over with an anti-static bag. Ink the poinsettia rubber stamp with a clear embossing inkpad by applying the inkpad to the stamp, rather than pressing the stamp into the inkpad. Press the stamp firmly onto the paper and lift off. Clean the stamp with damp kitchen paper.

May your Christmas be bright and beautiful

★ quick & clever ★

Watercolour paper is best, as it tolerates heat embossing well and takes the watercolour effect, but thick cartridge paper can be used instead – if making a batch of cards, test first.

step two Place the inked paper on scrap paper and sprinkle liberally with white embossing powder all over the stamped area – because the ink is clear, it is hard to see, so cover the whole area.

step three Hold the paper at the edges and tip the excess powder onto the scrap paper. Tap the back of the paper. Do not touch the area with powder on. Return the excess powder to the container.

May good fortune bloom for you this Christmas time

step four Place the paper on a tile or other heatproof surface and hold one corner with a wooden clothes peg. Heat the image with a heat gun until you see the powder turn semi-liquid as it melts.

step five Press a red inkpad onto a clean, white saucer or small plate to leave a residue of ink. Dip a fine paintbrush into a jar of water, then use to pick up the ink. Colour in the poinsettia petals – the embossed outline provides a boundary for the colour. Use green and brown inkpads to colour in the leaves and stalk.

step six Using a yellow glaze pen, colour in the centre of the flower with dots of colour. Ensure that the pen marks are dry before moving on to step seven.

step seven Place the paper on a flat surface. Lay a metal ruler along one edge, over the image, and hold down firmly with one hand. Tear the paper along the ruler towards you to create a torn edge. Tear the other edges in the same way. Alternatively, use a clear plastic rectangular template (see step seven, page 79). Mount the torn panel onto green card, then in turn onto the red single-fold card. Tie the ribbon around the spine of the card.

Tag it!

For a matching tag, the whole poinsettia image was embossed, as in the main card. The largest flower was then carefully cut out together with four leaves. Only the leaves were coloured in, with green ink applied with a damp fine paintbrush as before, then yellow glaze pen added to the centre of the flower. It was then mounted onto a textured red square single-fold card to set off the white of the flower.

quick & clever

If the poinsettia image for your main card goes slightly wrong, you can always cut out the good parts to use on a tag.

Ring Out the Bells

Self-adhesive motifs are very popular because not only are they quick to use and give dependable results but they are also surprisingly versatile. Available in a wide range, each design can be used in conjunction with foil, glitter, micro beads or Fun Flock to create numerous effects.

A subtle, sophisticated design is created by placing bell motifs on acetate, highlighting them in gold and mounting over white embossed paper, held in place at the spine with gold cord. A variation in the same colour scheme features motifs mounted behind apertures, while the third design sports a green glitter-enhanced single motif panel mounted with red brads.

✳ Window Shopping ✳

A series of three apertures was cut in a white embossed upright single-fold card using a Fiskars® ShapeTemplate™ and Fiskars® ShapeCutter™ tool, then acetate mounted behind the apertures with double-sided adhesive tape. A gift Magic Motif™ was placed in the centre of each aperture, then two covered with silver foil and the central one with gold. Four gold rub-on stars were then added to decorate the card.

✳ Sparkling Sprig ✳

A holly Magic Motif™ was placed in the centre of a square of acetate and then sprinkled with green ultra-fine glitter. The holly-decorated acetate panel was attached centrally to a square of white embossed card using a red brad in each corner. This panel was in turn mounted at the top of a dark green single-fold card, leaving a wider margin at the bottom of the card.

Ring Out the Bells

✳ ✳

You will need

* ✳ white embossed card 15 x 30cm (6 x 12in), folded in half
* ✳ acetate 15 x 30cm (6 x 12in), folded in half
* ✳ sheet of gold foil
* ✳ sheet of bells Magic Motifs™
* ✳ 30cm (12in) length of fine gold cord
* ✳ gold metallic sewing thread (optional)
* ✳ tapestry needle
* ✳ Basic Tool Kit (see page 8)

step one Choose three bell motifs from the sheet – here, two solid and one outline were used. Cut around each motif with a small pair of scissors, leaving a narrow margin.

✳ **quick & clever** ✳

You could add a rub-on festive message to the front of the acetate to personalize your card.

Ring out the bells for Christmas

step two Place the folded acetate on your cutting mat, aligning it with the grid printed on the mat. Take one bell motif and remove the white backing paper, leaving the transparent top layer in place. Place it on the acetate, using the grid as a guide. Press down all over the motif with your finger.

step three Carefully remove the transparent top layer from the motif, taking care not to touch the motif at this stage. Place the gold foil over the motif, with the gold side uppermost. Wrap clean kitchen paper around your finger and carefully press down on the gold sheet over the motif.

✳ ✳

step four Carefully peel away the foil, and as you do so, the motif will adhere to the foil. Repeat with the remaining motifs. It is easier to do each bell at a time rather than three in one go.

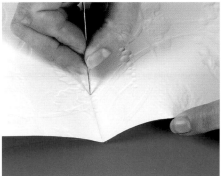

step five Place the folded white embossed card inside the acetate and place on a foam pad. Using a tapestry needle, pierce a hole in the spine 4cm (1½in) from the top and bottom edges through both the card and the acetate.

quick & clever ✴

If you have a little extra time to spare, emboss your own white card by using an embossing template (see Simply Snow, pages 28–31).

step six Thread the gold cord from the inside through each hole and tie in a reef knot in the centre of the spine of the card. Secure the ends of the cord with adhesive tape or bind with gold thread to prevent them unravelling.

quick & clever ✴

You can use narrow gold ribbon instead of gold cord – cut two slits in the spine to match the width of the ribbon.

Tag it!

For the matching tag, a single bell motif was placed on a circle of acetate and gold foil attached to it as in the main card. This was placed on top of a circle of white embossed card, which was then backed with another circle of acetate, and the three circles secured together with a gold brad. Any message can be added to the reverse of the embossed card and the tag attached to a gift with double-sided adhesive tape on the bottom acetate circle.

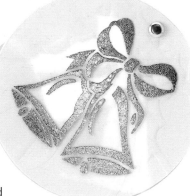

Rudolph the Reindeer

Pipe cleaners, in their original form, may be a relic from the past, but these fuzzy sticks in their contemporary reincarnation can be cut, bent and twisted to create wonderful shapes that will appeal to children and adults alike.

Here, they are used to fashion the antlers of a lovable reindeer on a novelty tag, which are then threaded with bells to jingle either on the card or when the tag is removed to hang on the tree. The reindeer's face is made in complementary soft-textured felt. The variation cards follow the escapades of old 'red-nose', as he falls down the chimney, or prances on his hindlegs and waves!

✶ Wrong-Footed Reindeer ✶

The reindeer's head was made as in the main card, but with two eyebrows drawn in and without bells on the antlers. Brown card was coloured with marker pen to resemble brick, then topped with white Fun Flock for snow. This was mounted over the reindeer's head onto a gold single-fold card. Brown felt was glued to pipe cleaner legs to resemble hooves. Three reindeer were punched and glued to the top of the card, with a length of cotton threaded with star sequins (see pages 34–35).

✶ Red-Nosed Reveller ✶

A whole reindeer is pictured here, without antlers (not all reindeers have them), waving a brown felt hoof attached to a length of brown pipe cleaner for an arm. The legs were made from pipe cleaners and felt in the same way, and the head as for the main card. A body was also cut from brown felt, with a red bow and bell attached at the neck. The reindeer was mounted onto cream card with a brown dashed-line border, then mounted onto a bronze single-fold card.

52

Rudolph the Reindeer

You will need

* brown and cream card 14 x 10cm (5½ x 4in)
* green single-fold card 15 x 10.5cm (6 x 4⅛in)
* brown and red felt 10cm (4in) square
* felt-tip pens – black, brown
* 2 wiggly eyes
* 2 brown pipe cleaners
* 4 small silver bells
* 6 small gold bells
* red craft wire
* round-nosed pliers
* Basic Tool Kit (see page 8)

Jingle all the way

step one Photocopy the reindeer's head template on page 108 onto paper and cut out. Draw around onto scrap card with a sharp HB pencil and cut out with a small pair of scissors (if making more than one card, keep one card cutout and use as a template). Glue the card reindeer's head to the brown felt with PVA (white) glue.

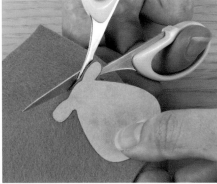

step two Cut the felt around the card reindeer's head with a small pair of scissors.

quick & clever

Pipe cleaners can be cut with scissors, but it is best to use pliers.

step three Cut a nose from red felt and glue in place. Attach two wiggly eyes with superglue. Draw in a mouth with a black felt-tip pen.

step four Thread a silver bell onto a 3cm (1⅛in) length of brown pipe cleaner. Repeat with another three lengths.

step five

Take one piece of pipe cleaner threaded with a bell and twist onto an 8cm (3⅛in) length of pipe cleaner without bells. Twist another short piece with a bell on just above the first.

step six
Cut a tag 12 x 6.5cm (4¾ x 2½in) from brown card (see pages 14–15) and one slightly smaller from cream card. Glue the cream tag onto the brown tag. With a brown felt-tip pen, draw a dashed line around the edge of the cream tag.

(see pages 14–15)

★ quick & clever ★

If you don't have any pipe cleaners or bells, cut antler shapes from card instead and give them a frosting with glitter glue.

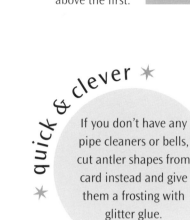

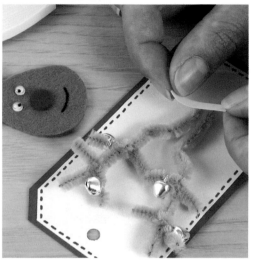

step seven
Attach the two antlers to the tag with double-sided adhesive tape. Place mini adhesive foam pads on the back of the reindeer's head and attach to the tag over the ends of the antlers.

step eight
Thread a 20cm (8in) length of red wire with the gold bells, twisting the wire after threading on each bell to keep in place, spaced apart. Make small loops in the wire between the bells. Thread the wire and bells through the hole in the tag. Secure the tag to the green single-fold card with repositional clear adhesive dots so that it can be removed by the recipient and hung on the tree.

Tag it!

Since reindeer accompany Father Christmas on his gift-delivering mission, this coordinating tag features a ready-made felt Santa's head. The head is glued onto a green card tag, decorated with a green dashed-line border around the edge. Instead of a regular holepunch, a star punch was used to make the hole in the top of the tag, through which green wire threaded with gold bells was passed.

Enjoy the Christmas sleigh-ride

Brilliant Baubles

The technique of pricking holes in card is deceptively easy and can be mastered in no time at all. It gives a subtle raised effect, which brings dimension and texture to these Eastern-inspired baubles.

Attractively shaped baubles are cut from gold, purple and mauve card for the main design, each embellished with an individual pricked pattern and enhanced with gold 3-D paint. The baubles appear to dangle from cord, drawn with silver pen, with two mounted using adhesive foam pads to add depth. As an even quicker alternative to cutting your own baubles using the templates provided, the variations show how die-cut shapes or a peel-off sticker can create similar designs.

✳ Pricked Patchwork ✳

A die-cutting tool and template were used to cut four identical baubles from silver and purple card. Using a single-needle pricking tool, the silver baubles were pricked with a zigzag pattern and the purple ones pricked with a wavy pattern, then the bauble tops coloured in with silver pen. The purple baubles were mounted onto squares of mauve card, then attached to a pink square single-fold card in opposite corners. The silver baubles were glued directly to the pink card.

✳ Silver Strung ✳

In this ultra-quick variation on the bauble theme, a silver outline peel-off sticker of a patterned bauble was attached to purple card. The shape was cut out around the outside edge, then the design on the bauble echoed with a pattern pricked with a single-needle pricking tool. The bauble was then hung with silver cord from a circular aperture cut in the centre of a pale purple single-fold card (see Spinning Angel, pages 64–67).

Brilliant Baubles

✳ ✳

You will need

* ✳ gold, purple and mauve card 10cm (4in) square
* ✳ white single-fold card 17.5 x 8cm (6⅞ x 3⅛in)
* ✳ gold 3-D paint
* ✳ silver pen
* ✳ 4-needle pricking tool
* ✳ single-needle pricking tool
* ✳ Basic Tool Kit (see page 8)

*Hang loose
and have a
happy Christmas*

step one Photocopy the four bauble templates on page 107 onto paper and cut out. Draw around onto the wrong side of the gold, purple and mauve card with a sharp HB pencil – bauble A on gold card, B on purple and C and D on mauve. (If making more than one card, draw around onto scrap card and cut out to make your own templates.)

✳ quick & clever ✳

You can design your own bauble shapes using real Christmas decorations as inspiration.

✳ quick & clever ✳

Card from an empty cereal box is ideal for using to make templates.

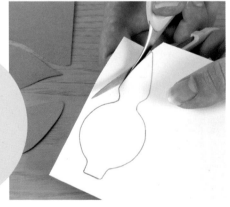

step two Cut around each of the baubles with a small pair of scissors. You may find it easier to cut roughly around each shape first, then cut out carefully.

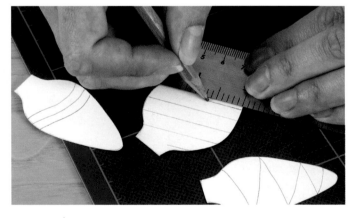

step three Place the baubles, white or wrong side up, on the cutting mat. Using a metal ruler and the pencil, draw diagonal lines across bauble A on the wrong side. Draw the patterns on the other baubles as shown on the templates on page 107.

✳ ✳

step four

Place bauble A, white or wrong side up, on a foam pad. Using the 4-needle pricking tool, prick holes along each of the lines. Try to make the pricks evenly spaced.

step five
Taking each of the remaining shapes in turn and using the single-needle pricking tool, prick holes along each of the lines. Again, ensure that the holes are evenly spaced.

step six
Turn all the baubles right side up. Add two wavy lines of gold 3-D paint across the top of each bauble. On baubles C and D, add dots of the paint below the lines of pricked holes, and on B, add a dot of the paint in the centre of each star shape. Leave the paint to dry.

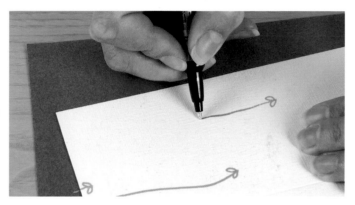

step seven
Open out the white single-fold card and place on scrap paper. Using the silver pen, draw lines to resemble strings for each bauble. You can make a light pencil line first, but use a fluid movement with the pen and continue off the card onto the scrap paper. Draw small loops at the end of each line for bows.

step eight
Glue baubles C and D directly to the white card adjoining the bows. Attach baubles A and B to the card using adhesive foam pads.

Tag it!

For a bauble tag, two red card circles were cut using a shape cutter. Using the single-needle tool, a pattern of holes was pricked from the reverse side of one of the card circles. The red side was then decorated with silver pen in lines of dots. The second card circle was glued to the back of the first and silver card added for the bauble top. A hole was punched through the top with a mini holepunch, then silver organza ribbon threaded through and tied in a bow.

✳ ✳

Winter Welcome

For this collection, intricate wreath shapes, pre-cut by a laser, are used to make a threesome of traditional-style cards. The Victorians are often credited with introducing the custom of hanging wreaths on front doors. More recently, these once formal, evergreen decorations have taken on added glitz and glamour.

The main card design captures all the luxuriance of a wreath's greenery, as well as the welcoming cheer it bestows upon the entrance to a home. A simple door background is created using coloured pens, on which the wreath, made up of two layers for extra dimension, is mounted. Equally effective are the two variations that feature just a single wreath layer. Tartan ribbon brings a Scottish flourish to a larger wreath motif on one card, while on the other, selected leaves are coloured gold for an opulent look and the wreath shape hung within a circular aperture.

✳ Tartan Tidings ✳

A single wreath was glued to a pale green single-fold card with PVA (white) glue. A bow was tied from red tartan ribbon and attached with double-sided adhesive tape. The wreath was embellished with gemstones and glitter glue. Lengths of tartan ribbon were attached along the four edges of the card with double-sided adhesive tape and secured on the reverse with tape. A clear gemstone was added to each corner with superglue to finish.

✳ Gold Leaf Splendour ✳

A circular aperture was cut in a red single-fold card and green card attached to the back inside panel. The larger leaves of a wreath and corner garlands were coloured with a gold marker pen. The corner garlands were glued around the aperture, and a robin peel-off sticker added. The wreath was embellished with gemstones, then hung using invisible thread secured on the inside with tape. The bow was attached with double-sided adhesive tape.

Winter Welcome

You will need

- ✶ light green card 13.5 x 7cm (5¼ x 2¾in)
- ✶ gold card 5mm x 2.5cm (³⁄₁₆ x 1in)
- ✶ green single-fold card 15 x 10.5cm (6 x 4¼in)
- ✶ 2 sheets of Rayher® laser-cut wreaths
- ✶ silver marker pen
- ✶ light beige felt-tip pen
- ✶ 3 green medium gemstones
- ✶ 3 clear and 2 green small gemstones
- ✶ 1 green brad
- ✶ 20cm (8in) length of red narrow ribbon
- ✶ silicone adhesive
- ✶ Basic Tool Kit (see page 8)

Christmas celebrations begin at your doorstep

step one Each wreath on the laser-cut sheets is held in place by small, uncut pieces of paper. Use a small pair of scissors to snip these uncut strands, releasing the wreath shapes from the sheets. Trim any small strands of paper where the wreaths were attached. Cut two dark green wreaths of the same size.

quick & clever ✶

Silicone adhesive is used in step two because it dries clear and so becomes almost invisible. It can take a while to dry, so use mini foam adhesive pads or clear adhesive dots for a faster alternative.

step two
Place three small blobs of silicone adhesive at evenly spaced intervals around one wreath. Add glue to the larger leaf shapes. Place the second wreath directly on top of the first and put to one side for the glue to dry.

step three Attach three green medium gemstones to the wreath with superglue, taking great care not to get the glue on your hands (some gemstones are self-adhesive, so there is no need to add glue). Glue three clear and two green small gemstones to the wreath.

Why not personalize the door by adding the number or house name of the recipient? You could even add a special seasonal message poking through the letterbox.

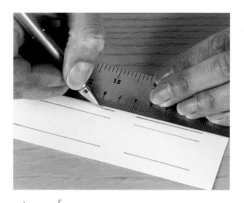

step four Use the template on page 107 to draw the door panels on the light green card with a silver marker pen and ruler – it is best to use a ruler with a raised edge to avoid smudging the ink.

step five Go over the silver with a light beige felt-tip pen to create a shadow effect – this is best done freehand for a realistic result, but if you don't feel sufficiently confident, you can use a ruler if you wish.

step six Punch a hole with a mini holepunch close to and in the centre of one side of the light green card. Insert a green brad from the right side and bend the brad 'wings' outwards to flatten on the reverse side. Glue the gold card to the centre of the door, to form the letterbox, then mount the door onto the green single-fold card. Place small dots of PVA (white) glue all over the underside of the lower-level wreath and attach to the top of the door.

step seven Tie the red ribbon in a double-loop bow (see page 13). Attach the bow to the top of the wreath with double-sided adhesive tape and secure the ends of the ribbon in place with more tape. You may need to trim the ends of the ribbon. Here, one end of the ribbon was threaded through the two layers of wreath, but this is optional.

Tag it!

For this quick tag to coordinate with the main card, three lighter green wreaths were glued together with PVA (white) glue. The wreath was mounted onto a square of pale green card and then onto a red square single-fold card. Gemstones were glued around the wreath and in each corner of the green card with superglue. A bow was made from green ribbon and attached to the wreath as in step seven of the main card.

Hang up some holiday cheer

Spinning Angel

Rubber stamping is a versatile craft that can be taken to its limits in a variety of directions, as demonstrated here, where a single stamp has been applied in different ways to create a surprisingly diverse range of designs.

In the main design, a cute angel image, coloured in with marker pens, is mounted on a circle of card suspended in an aperture, to give the impression of hovering in the heavens. The same stamp, printed twice, is presented on a watercolour-effect background for contrast in the second design, and then used to create an all-over pattern with the fading-out technique for the final card.

✳ Angelic Duo ✳

The angel stamp was inked with a clear embossing inkpad and printed twice, one just above the other, onto watercolour card, then sprinkled with white embossing powder and heated (see Pretty Poinsettias, pages 44–47). The angels' faces, hair and halos were coloured in with pens, then a watercolour effect applied to the background using blue ink from an inkpad diluted with water and a fine paintbrush. This stamped panel was mounted onto a turquoise card, then ribbon tied through the spine and around the base.

✳ Just Heavenly ✳

The fading-out technique (see page 11) was used to print the angel over a pink single-fold card, then the halos coloured in with gold pen. A darker pink card circle was mounted in the centre. An angel was printed onto white card using black StazOn™ ink, coloured in and cut out with a narrow margin, then glued to the circle. Tree and star sequins were threaded onto white fibre thread with a large sewing needle, then the thread tied around the card spine with a bow at the top.

Spinning Angel

✳✳✳✳✳✳✳✳✳✳✳✳✳✳✳✳✳✳✳✳✳✳✳✳

You will need

* white card 10 x 15cm (4 x 6in)
* pale blue card 13cm (5in) square
* pale blue single-fold card 12cm (4¾in) square
* angel rubber stamp
* black StazOn™ inkpad and StazOn™ cleaner
* dual-tip marker pens – blush, pastel blue
* yellow glaze pen
* gold pen
* pink felt-tip pen
* silver star peel-off stickers
* 35cm (13¾in) length of blue fibre thread
* Fiskars® circle ShapeTemplate™ and Fiskars® ShapeCutter™ tool
* Basic Tool Kit (see page 8)

step one Place the white card on a clean, flat surface. Ink the angel stamp with the black StazOn™ inkpad and then print onto the white card – StazOn™ is recommended so that it does not bleed with the pens. Do not print too close to the edge of the card. Clean your stamp immediately with the StazOn™ cleaner and kitchen paper.

May your Christmas be heavenly happy

step two Using the blush dual-tip marker pen, colour in the angel's face, neck, hands and feet. Apply the pen lightly, as the card will absorb the colour from the pen. Colour in the hair with the yellow glaze pen, the halo with the gold pen and the dress trim with the pink felt-tip pen.

step three With the thick end of the pastel blue dual-tip marker pen, colour around the angel. Work quickly and do not try to colour too close to the angel. Colour in a significant area around the angel.

✳✳✳✳✳✳✳✳✳✳✳✳✳✳✳✳✳✳✳✳✳✳✳✳✳✳✳✳✳✳

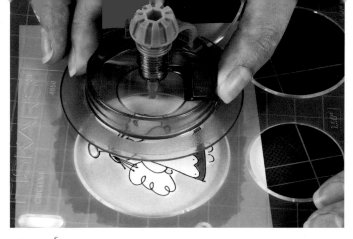

step four Place the white card on a cutting mat, then position the Fiskars® circle ShapeTemplate™ over the angel, selecting the 6.2cm (2½in) diameter circle. Use the Fiskars® ShapeCutter™ tool to cut around the circle template.

✱ quick & clever ✱

A special message or even a photo could be placed on the reverse side of the card circle instead of the star stickers.

step five Cut another circle the same size from the pale blue card. If you wish, colour in more white card with the marker pen, then cut out. Open the blue single-fold card out and place on the cutting mat. Use the 7.6cm (3in) diameter template to cut a circle in the front panel centre.

step six Decorate the reverse side of the blue card circle with silver star peel-off stickers. Tie the fibre thread around the front panel, down the centre of the aperture, then tie in a bow at the top. If the length is too long, trim the ends.

step seven Place double-sided adhesive tape on the blue circle and position under the fibre. Position the angel circle directly over the blue circle and press together so that the fibre is sandwiched in between.

Tag it!

To make this coordinating tag, the same angel stamp was printed onto white card using pink ink. The shape was cut out, but the halo trimmed off, and then coloured in with dual-tip marker pens – the dress in pink, the hair in brown and the face in light pink. The angel was then glued to a pink tag card and a halo drawn in with gold pen. A hole was punched in the top with a mini holepunch, then white fibre thread threaded through and tied in a knot.

Santas Galore

Embossed peel-off stickers bring an instant professional quality to a design, especially when presented on a card with a more unusual construction than the standard single fold and with an extra textural dimension.

The main card is folded concertina-style, then covered with torn strips of tissue paper and decorated with glitter glue. This provides a sparkling snowscape for a Santa and sleigh embossed peel-off sticker attached to the front fold. The variation designs, again featuring Santa stickers, take a short-cut in using pre-cut cards, but in the first instance trimmed to create an asymmetrical fold and in the second covered with metallic-flecked tissue.

✳ Santa's Star Turn ✳

The front panel of a single-fold card was trimmed in width, then a torn rectangle of green handmade tissue paper glued to it. A Father Christmas embossed peel-off sticker was placed on top, then three embossed star stickers in decreasing sizes were attached to the exposed back panel of the card. Small dots of green glitter glue were added around the stars and to the four corners of the front panel to finish.

✳ Santa's Special Delivery ✳

A white single-fold card was covered with torn strips of white tissue paper incorporating flecks of gold and silver. Another Father Christmas embossed peel-off sticker was placed on white card and cut out with a small pair of scissors, then mounted centrally on the front of the covered card using adhesive foam pads to add dimension. Dots of silver glitter glue were added all over the background for a snowy feel.

Santas Galore

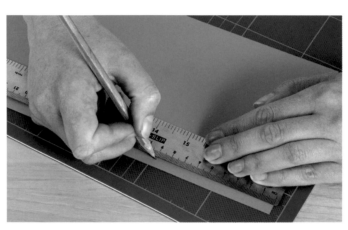

You will need

* blue card 15 x 28cm (6 x 11in)
* sheet of blue tissue or handmade paper flecked with gold
* white card 12 x 15cm (4¾ x 6in)
* embossed Father Christmas peel-off sticker
* blue glitter glue
* Basic Tool Kit (see page 8)

step one Place the blue card on a cutting mat. With a metal ruler and a sharp HB pencil, mark 5cm (2in) and 19cm (7½in) from the left-hand short edge along the top of the card and again along the bottom. Turn the card over and mark 10cm (4in) from what is now the right-hand short edge top and bottom.

step two Turn the card back over and align the metal ruler with the top and bottom pencil marks 5cm (2in) from the left-hand edge. Using a scoring tool (see page 8), score along the ruler right across the card. Repeat at the 19cm (7½in) pencil marks. Turn the card over and score across the card at the 10cm (4in) pencil marks.

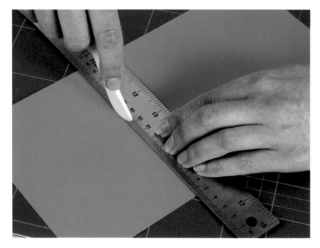

Santa Claus
is coming
to town

step three Fold along the two outer score lines so that the score lines lie inside the folds, then turn the card over to fold the inner line. Keeping the card on the cutting mat, press along the creases firmly with the flat edge of a bone folder.

step four Find the grain of the tissue or handmade paper you are using and tear strips approximately 17cm (6¾in) long and 2cm (¾in) wide. Some handmade paper may not have a grain, so experiment. The strips will be longer than the card, but this is OK.

step five Using a glue stick, apply glue to the card, then place the torn tissue strips onto the glue – it is easier to apply glue to the card than to the delicate tissue. Cover both front and rear panels with tissue, making sure that the strips overhang the edges. Using a medium-sized pair of scissors, trim the ends of the tissue to align with the card.

★ quick & clever ★

Store glitter glues upside down so that the liquid is already at the nozzle and there are no air bubbles.

step six Carefully remove the Father Christmas sticker and place on the white card – when removing an intricate solid sticker from its backing, ease it off carefully or it may tear. Using a small pair of scissors or a craft knife, cut around the edge of the sticker carefully so as not to leave any white card showing.

step seven Place PVA (white) glue just along the bottom of the reverse side of the Father Christmas and attach to the front flap. Add small dots of the glitter glue all over the front two panels of the card. Leave to dry.

Tag it!

This interestingly shaped gift tag, folded to create a narrow front (side) panel, also features an embossed peel-off sticker, in this case an invitingly wrapped Christmas gift box. It was applied to the back panel of the folded green card, then dots of white glitter glue used to decorate the side panel of the tag.

By Candle Light

Candles symbolizing hope and love at Christmas are given pride of place in these cards. Floral decorations make a fitting accompaniment, here quickly and cleverly re-created in paper using the technique of fringed quilling.

In the main design, parchment-backed apertures permit suffused light to highlight the candles framed within. Holly leaves grouped around sparkly flowers are scored and shaped to give a naturalistic 3-D effect. The same leaves and fringed flowers, this time in traditional red, adorn a single candle in a simplified version of the main card, and are used again to enhance a group of candles with strips of music score in a carol singing-inspired design.

✶ A Christmas Carol ✶

Two strips of old music score were torn and attached to a purple single-fold card using no-set eyelets. Five candle shapes were cut from purple metallic paper and attached to the card, then topped with yellow card flames, the centres coloured with orange felt-tip pen. Three fringed quilled flowers were made from gold 1cm (⅜in) wide paper strip and interspersed among holly leaves, cut as for the main card.

✶ Flame Frame ✶

A single candle shape was cut from gold card and mounted onto a strip of purple card, with a yellow card flame added. This is turn was mounted onto a mauve single-fold card. The holly leaves were cut using a die-cutting template and tool, then scored and shaped as for the main card and glued to the base of the candle. Fringed quilled flowers were made from red metallic 1cm (⅜in) wide paper strip and attached to the leaves.

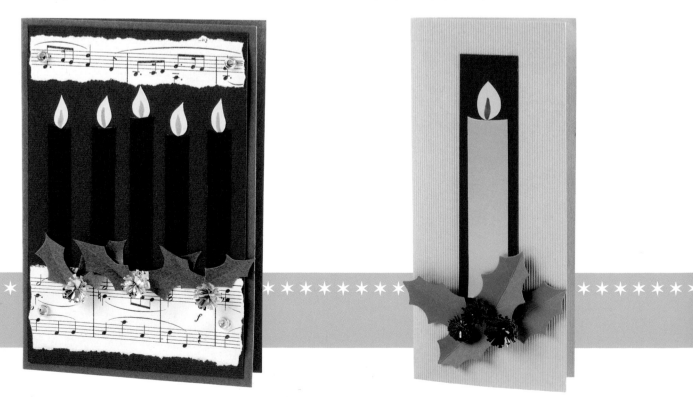

By Candle Light

You will need

* purple single-fold card 14cm (5½in) square
* parchment paper 12 x 13cm (4¾ x 5in)
* red and purple metallic 1cm (⅜in) wide paper strip
* yellow card 5cm (2in) square
* dark green card 10cm (4in) square
* orange felt-tip pen
* small ball embossing tool
* fringing tool
* quilling tool
* Basic Tool Kit (see page 8)

step one Open out the purple single-fold card and place, wrong side up, on a cutting mat. Measure and mark out three apertures 2cm (¾in), 3cm (1⅛in) and 2cm (¾in) wide by 9cm (3½in) high with a metal ruler and sharp HB pencil on the card front. Cut out with the ruler and a craft knife.

step two Place double-sided adhesive tape all round the apertures and either side of the central aperture. Remove the backing and place the parchment paper over the top.

quick & clever

When cutting the apertures in the card front, turn the card as you cut so that you always draw the knife towards you.

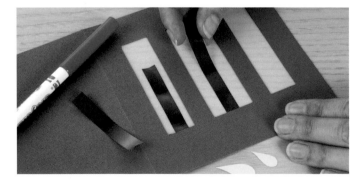

step three Turn the card over. Cut three 7cm (2¾in) lengths of red paper strip. Cut a curve in the tops and trim the lengths to graduate in size. Attach one to each parchment panel, tucking each bottom end under the purple card. Cut three flames from yellow card. Colour the centres with an orange felt-tip pen.

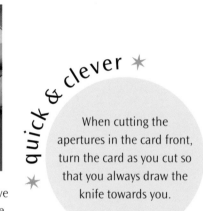

step four Photocopy the holly leaf template on page 108 onto paper and cut out. Draw around onto dark green card six times with a sharp HB pencil and cut out with a small pair of scissors. Alternatively, use a punch or die-cut. Place one holly leaf on a cutting mat. Using a small ball embossing tool, score a line down the centre and then small lines outwards from the central line. Use your fingers to curl the leaf slightly. Repeat with the other holly leaves.

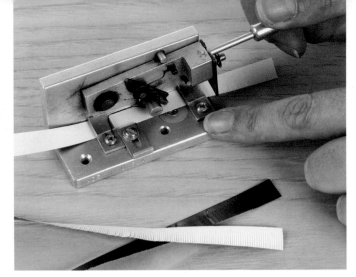

step five

Insert a 40cm (15¾in) length of purple paper strip, metallic side down, into the fringing tool. Move the handle up and down to draw the paper through the tool. Repeat with a second length.

★ quick & clever ★

If you don't have a fringing tool, you can cut strips of paper with a small pair of scissors. Hold the edge of the paper with a bulldog clip while cutting, and remember not to snip all the way across.

step six

Cut four 15cm (6in) lengths of the fringed paper. Trim about 2mm (³⁄₃₂in) off the fringed edge to make the flowers a little smaller.

step seven

Insert one end of a fringed length of paper through the prongs of a quilling tool. Rotate the tool, making sure that the metallic side is facing inwards.

Tag it!

The accompanying tag breaks with tradition in shape, but retains the customary colour scheme, the card layered red on dark green. Two fringed quilled flowers were made from silver 1cm (³⁄₈in) wide paper strip, with three holly leaves cut, scored and shaped as for the main card, then attached to the tag. A hole was punched in the top of the tag with a mini holepunch, then a length of purple narrow ribbon threaded through and tied in a shoestring bow.

step eight

Continue rotating until the end of the paper is reached, then apply a dot of PVA (white) glue to the end. Hold against the coil for a few seconds while the glue dries. Spread out the fringes with your fingers. Repeat with the other fringed lengths of paper. Attach the leaves and the flowers to the purple card as shown in the main card photo.

Bringing you the warming glow of our festive greetings

Across the Miles

When posting a card to family or friends abroad, the weight needs to be kept to a minimum, so here the letter has been cleverly incorporated into the card. The folded lightweight paper is sandwiched between two outer pieces of card, one decorated with a sponged smiley snowman.

White acrylic paint was used to sponge a snowman shape onto card for the main design. Glaze pens were used to add facial details and patterned paper for a plaid scarf. The variations illustrate how different shapes of snowman can be quickly created, and the fun to be had decorating them as you might a real one.

★ Winter Warmer ★

This tall snowman was sponged as in the main card, and twiggy arms added using the same pearl white paint applied with a fine paintbrush. The eyes and nose were coloured in using glaze pens. The scarf and hat were cut from red and white striped paper, then a mini letter made from folded cream paper, with a drawn address and stamp. The heart was punched from red card. The dark blue snowman panel was then mounted onto snowflake-printed card.

★ Snow Pal ★

This jolly snowman's body was sponged as before, with the facial features and arms added in glaze pen. The hat was cut from patterned paper, and the mittens, birds and holly sprigs all cut from a booklet of printed papers. The blue snowman panel was mounted onto blue-checked paper and then in turn onto a bright blue single-fold card, decorated with a bird and holly sprig glued in the bottom right-hand corner.

Across the Miles

You will need

* blue lightweight paper 18 x 29cm (7 x 11½in)
* 2 pieces of dark blue card 18 x 8cm (7 x 3⅛in)
* blue card 21 x 14cm (8¼ x 5½in)
* scrap of patterned paper
* acrylic paint – pearl white, sapphire blue (optional)
* glaze pens – orange, black, brown
* clear plastic rectangular tearing template (optional)
* sponge dauber or small piece of clean sponge
* Basic Tool Kit (see page 8)

May your holidays be filled with fun and laughter

step one Fold the blue lightweight paper in half. If you are using heavier paper, follow the instructions for scoring and folding on page 9. With the flat edge of a bone folder, press along the fold to make a sharp crease. (You may want to write your letter before folding the paper.)

step two Fold back one short edge to the centre fold. Crease this edge with the bone folder. Turn the paper over, fold the other short edge to the centre fold and press with the bone folder. You now have a concertina.

★ quick & clever ★

Trim the spine off a tall dark blue single-fold card to make two separate pieces of card the same size in one go.

step three Rub a glue stick along one of the shorter edges of the blue paper and then attach to one of the pieces of dark blue card. (The card used here is blue on one side only, so the paper is attached to the reverse side, which is white.) Attach the other piece of dark blue card to the other end of the paper, blue side facing outwards.

step four Place a small amount of white acrylic paint on a clean, plain saucer. With a sponge dauber or piece of sponge, pick up small amounts of the paint and gently dab in the centre of the blue card to create three rounds, building up the shape from the centre outwards. Practise on scrap paper first to gauge how much paint is needed on the dauber or sponge.

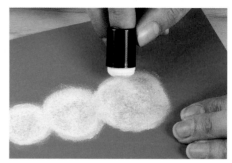

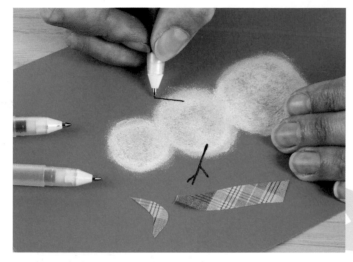

step five Here, sapphire blue acrylic paint was then sponged on top of the white for a sparkly effect, but this is optional. Leave the paint to dry according to the manufacturer's instructions.

step six Using the glaze pens, add a carrot-shaped nose in orange, and eyes, mouth and buttons in black. Use the brown pen to draw in stick arms. Cut a scarf shape from two pieces of patterned paper. Leave the pen marks to dry.

Tag it!

Mittens are the essential accompaniment to making a real snowman, so here they are used on a coordinating tag. Two were die-cut from tartan paper, and a green trim added. They were then glued to a bright blue tag, with a fluffy snowball glued between them. Sapphire blue acrylic paint was applied all round the edges of the tag, a hole punched in the top with a regular office holepunch and tartan narrow ribbon threaded through, secured with a knot.

step seven For a torn effect, a clear plastic rectangular template was used as an alternative to a metal ruler, as this allows you to tear all four edges easily. Position the clear template over the snowman, hold firmly in place with one hand and tear the paper along the edges of the template with the other hand. If the template is smaller than your image, just move it down as you tear. Glue the snowman panel to the front dark blue card.

Fantasy Greetings

Christmas is the perfect opportunity to indulge in the sparkliest, shiniest materials available, while punches provide a quick way of making identical festive shapes for creating clever, contemporary-style cards.

Here, Fantasy Fiber™, chosen for its iridescent shine, is fused into a single sheet by heating with an iron and then punched. In the main design, the negative Christmas-tree shapes left after punching and a punched-out shape are combined, the latter framed within a metal tag to provide the focus. For a speedier variation, just the negative tree shape is placed in the metal tag, and the final card combines a row of punched-out shapes with the negative shape in a tag.

✶ Vision in Pink ✶

A single tree was punched from deep pink fused Fantasy Fiber™ and the negative shape attached to a square of pale pink card. This was then inserted into a large, square metal tag rim and crimped, as for the main card. Sheer pink ribbon was threaded through and tied in a knot at the top of the tag, then the tag attached to a pale pink square single-fold card with double-sided adhesive tape.

✶ Wonder Windows ✶

Three tree shapes were punched from deep pink fused Fantasy Fiber™, square resin stickers placed over the trees, then glued to a mauve single-fold card. White Fantasy Fiber™ was fused and cut to fit inside a large, square metal tag rim. The negative shape was cut to the same size and both pieces crimped in the tag. White organza and pale purple ribbon were wrapped around the card.

80

Fantasy Greetings

You will need

* ✳ mauve card 8cm (3¼in) square
* ✳ purple card 12.5cm (4⅞in) square
* ✳ mauve single-fold card 13.5cm (5¼in) square
* ✳ purple Fantasy Fiber™
* ✳ Christmas tree punch
* ✳ crimping tool, metal tag rim 4cm (1½in) square and matching template
* ✳ 20cm (8in) length of purple ribbon
* ✳ baking paper
* ✳ iron
* ✳ Basic Tool Kit (see page 8)

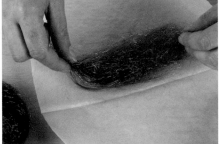

step one Place the baking paper on a heatproof surface such as an ironing board. Spread the Fantasy Fiber™ out on the baking paper so that the fibres form a long strip.

step two Fold the baking paper over to cover the fibres. Follow the manufacturer's instructions for the Fantasy Fiber™ and set the iron to the appropriate setting. Press firmly with the iron over the whole strip of fibres for 3–5 seconds, or according to the instructions.

step three The heat from the iron will fuse the fibres together to form a thin continuous sheet. Lift off the baking paper and check that the fibres have fused together. Peel away the strip of fused fibres from the baking paper. Make a second strip of fused fibres in the same way.

✳ quick & clever ✳

Different colours of fibres can be mixed together to create new colours. Experiment with the bonding procedure, but always follow the manufacturer's instructions.

step four Place one strip of fused fibres in the tree punch and press down. Here, the punch was held upside down so that the positioning of the strip of fibres could be checked. Move the punch along and punch again to make a second punched-out tree shape next to the first. Position the punch on the other side of the first punched-out shape and punch again. Repeat with the other strip of fused fibres.

step five Place the mauve square of card on a cutting mat and place the plastic tag template on top. Draw around the central square with a pencil. Cut out the small square from the mauve card with a small pair of scissors.

Have a sparkling Christmas

step six Place the small mauve card square into the tag rim, then insert into the crimping tool. Squeeze the handle of the tool to secure the rim around the card, then remove the tag. Stick one of the punched-out trees to the tag centre with PVA (white) glue.

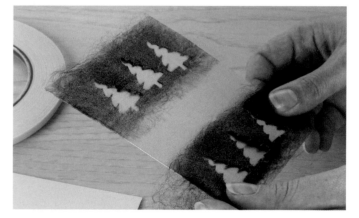

step seven Position one punched strip across the top of the purple card, fold the ends around the edges and secure to the reverse with double-sided adhesive tape. Secure the other strip across the bottom. Mount onto the mauve single-fold card. Tie a knot in either end of the ribbon and secure across the centre, then attach the tag with double-sided adhesive tape.

Tag it!

Making a tag is a great way to use up leftovers. Here, spare pieces of the fused fibres were cut and attached to the top and bottom of an upright rectangular-shaped piece of pale pink card. A punched-out tree shape was glued to the centre, then a hole punched at the top with a mini holepunch, a length of sheer pink ribbon threaded through and tied in a knot.

quick & clever

If you don't have a tree-shaped punch, you can cut out shapes with a small pair of scissors.

May your Christmas shine and sparkle

Hang Out the Stockings

A die-cutting system may be relatively costly, but this collection of cards demonstrates the impressive return you can get on your investment from just one die-cut shape of a stocking. Christmas stockings hung near chimneys symbolize the high expectations we have and also evoke fond childhood memories.

The printed papers used in the main card re-create the rich colours and patterns of folk-style fabrics for a homely festive feel. The white Fun Flock adds an appealing three-dimensional element to the stockings, while the simply stitched, punched hearts bring a loving touch to all three designs. A quick variation was made by using coordinated patterned papers in a single colour scheme, embellished with bows and hearts. The approach was then taken further by adding tiny bells to the stocking and cutting out toy shapes for an equally appealing effect.

✳ All Lined Up ✳

This ultra-quick variation creates an illusion of stitching on the punched hearts with silver marker pen. The stockings were cut and embellished with Fun Flock and attached to a pale green single-fold card. A line was drawn with the silver pen across the top of the card and four green bows added. The hearts were punched from the same pale green card as the base card, with dashed lines drawn around the edges and a cross in the centre with the silver pen. A heart was then glued to the centre of each stocking.

✳ Stocking Surprise ✳

A stocking was die-cut from red handmade paper, with a white toe and heel attached. The stocking top was cut freehand, white Fun Flock added and tiny bells sewn on. Toys and candy canes cut from printed papers were glued to pale green card first, then the stocking glued over the top and holly added. The panel was mounted onto a dark green single-fold card and stitched hearts glued to the corners.

Hang Out the Stockings

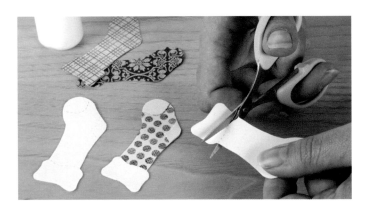

You will need

* 3 complementary patterned papers for the stockings, 10 x 5cm (4 x 2in) each
* white card 10 x 21cm (4 x 8¼in)
* patterned paper 11 x 13.5cm (4¼ x 5¼in), plus extra scraps
* burgundy card 10 x 12.5cm (4 x 4⅞in), plus extra scraps
* cream single-fold card 14.5cm (5¾in) square
* white Fun Flock
* wooden mini pegs
* 20cm (8in) length of green ribbon
* die-cutting tool and stocking die-cut
* corner rounder punch
* heart punch
* sewing needle and beige sewing thread
* Basic Tool Kit (see page 8)

SAFETY NOTE: Asthmatics should avoid using Fun Flock because of its tiny fibres.

Sending you stockingfuls of love for Christmas

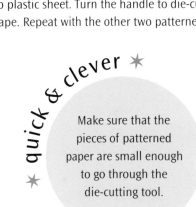

step one Place the base plastic sheet and stocking die-cut in the die-cutting tool. Position one of the three patterned papers, printed side up, over the die-cut. Add the top plastic sheet. Turn the handle to die-cut the stocking shape. Repeat with the other two patterned papers.

step two Use the white card to die-cut three more plain stocking shapes, one at a time. Cut around the perforations at the top, toe and heel with a small pair of scissors, then attach the white card pieces to the patterned stockings.

quick & clever ✶

Make sure that the pieces of patterned paper are small enough to go through the die-cutting tool.

step three Spread a generous amount of PVA (white) glue all over the white areas of the stockings.

step four

Place the stockings on scrap paper and sprinkle white Fun Flock over the glue, making sure that all the glued areas are covered. Leave for 1 minute and then shake off the excess flock and return it to the jar.

step five

Take the corner rounder punch and punch each of the corners of the remaining patterned paper and the burgundy card. Attach the patterned paper to the cream single-fold card and then the burgundy card to the patterned paper.

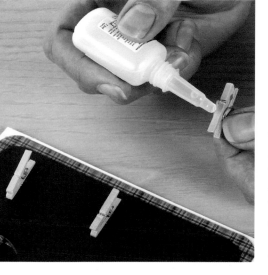

step six

Place superglue along one side of a mini peg. Attach close to one end of the burgundy card at the top Attach the other two pegs evenly spaced. Tie a knot at either end of the ribbon and thread through the pegs.

step seven

Punch two hearts from the scraps of burgundy card and one from the scraps of patterned paper.

step eight

Prick two holes in each heart with the needle thread with a double length of the beige thread. Take the thread through the holes and tie in a double knot on the front. Trim the ends. Glue the hearts in a row to the bottom right-hand corner of the cream card.

Tag it!

A quick tag to accompany the card was made using a green paper for the stocking top, toe and heel instead of Fun Flock. A small piece of green ribbon was attached to the stocking top in a loop, then the whole stocking mounted onto cream card with the corners rounded. A piece of ribbon was wrapped around the bottom of the cream card and secured in place on the reverse side. Three punched hearts were glued across the ribbon and then the cream card mounted onto green patterned card. A small piece of cream card was attached to the top, with green ribbon threaded through. A heart was stitched to either end of the ribbon.

Ice Skating Fun

This group of coordinated cards, featuring peel-off stickers of a hat, mitts and skates, perfectly illustrates how a simple craft technique can be both clever and quick. A welcome warmth is brought to this ever-popular winter sport through the use of soft blue and pink colours.

In the main design, the stickers provide the outline of the shapes, which are then cut from white card. This framework is then coloured in with felt-tip and sparkly glitter pens. The pens are subsequently used to create backgrounds alive with swirling motion, convincingly conveying the skating action. The variation cards are tailored either for a girl or a boy by focusing on a single motif of the skates and hat respectively, combined with the appropriate, traditional colour scheme.

✳ Pink for a Girl ✳

A pair of pink ice skates makes an ideal image for a stylistic girlie card. A skates white peel-off sticker was mounted onto white card and cut out, then coloured in pink with felt-tip and glitter pens, the blades in grey. Pieces of leftover white sticker were added for toes, heels and tongues. The skates were then attached to pink card, with a brad inserted into each corner. The panel was mounted onto a paler pink single-fold card, decorated with the pens, with adhesive foam pads.

✳ Blue for a Boy ✳

The hat motif has a novelty appeal for boys. A blue single-fold card was decorated with wavy lines drawn with felt-tip and glitter pens. Snowflake peel-off stickers were attached at random, with some going over the card edges. A hat black peel-off sticker was attached to white card and cut out. Details were coloured in with the pens, and the hat attached to the card centre with adhesive foam pads. The bobble was secured in place using PVA (white) glue.

Ice Skating Fun

You will need

* white card 10 x 21cm (4 x 8¼in)
* blue single-fold card 8 x 20cm (3⅛ x 8in), fold at the top
* skating black outline peel-off stickers
* felt-tip pens
* glitter pens
* Basic Tool Kit (see page 8)

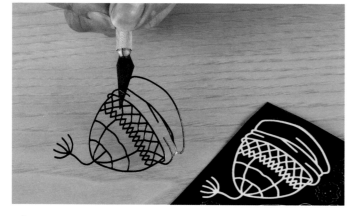

step one Remove the hat peel-off sticker from the sheet of stickers with a craft knife and let it spring back into shape. Ensure that all the inner pieces of sticker are removed at this point.

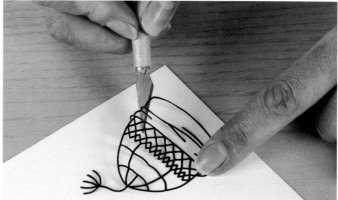

step two Place the sticker on the white card, one end down first, and press down with your finger, then let the rest of the sticker fall down onto the card. This helps to avoid distorting the sticker. Repeat with the skates and mitts stickers.

step three

Cut around all three shapes with a small pair of scissors. Try to cut close to the sticker edge to ensure that there is no background card visible. If you accidentally cut into the edge of the sticker slightly, just continue and keep a smooth edge. Here, a fine, delicate part of the laces is carefully lifted up and the card cut underneath.

quick & clever

Outline peel-off stickers come in many colours, including gold and silver. You can also change the colour of the outlines by using permanent marker pens.

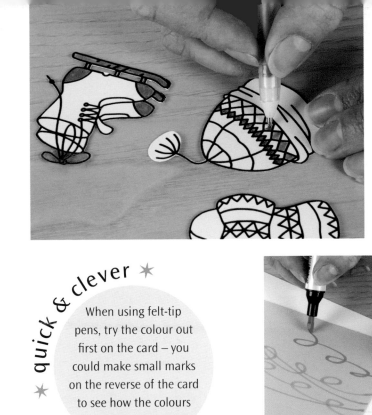

step four Colour in the stickers using felt-tip and glitter pens. Leave some areas blank so that the white card shows through. You may want to colour in using felt-tip pen first and then go over the same area with a glitter pen for a different colour.

Warmest thoughts and wishes to you and your family

quick & clever ✶

When using felt-tip pens, try the colour out first on the card – you could make small marks on the reverse of the card to see how the colours work together.

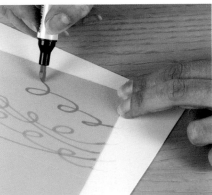

step five Place the blue single-fold card on scrap paper and make swirls all over the card, going over the edges onto the scrap paper, with a thick blue felt-tip pen. Make smooth, fluid movements with the pen for a continuous and even colour. If you stop and leave the pen on the card, you will leave a blob of colour.

step six Go over some swirls with a blue glitter pen to create a feel of freshly cut ice and to give dimension to the background. The glitter pen is finer than the felt-tip pen, so just draw a fine line following the swirls. By using blue pens on blue card, the background does not dominate the card.

step seven Glue the shapes to the card with PVA (white) glue, placing the skates in the centre and the mitts and hat either side.

Tag it!

A simple yet effective tag was made using just the skates peel-off sticker. The sticker was cut out and mounted onto white card, then the blades only coloured in with grey felt-tip pen. The motif was mounted onto blue paper, cut into a tag shape and decorated with swirls as in steps five and six of the main card. The paper was mounted onto a slightly larger tag shape cut from darker blue card. A hole was punched in the top with a mini holepunch, white ribbons and threads threaded through and tied in a knot.

There Came Three Kings

The traditional craft of paper quilling, in which narrow strips of paper are coiled with a quilling tool, is used to create these cutting-edge crown designs. In this instance, the paper strips are edged with bronze, for a festive twist.

The main design sets a red crown against a gold background for a luxurious feel, the quilled coils making eye-catching embellishments for the crown points. The same stylized motif and technique is applied in other ways to achieve quite different yet equally effective results – in a silver crown trio, enhanced with a pricked border and gemstones, or as a crown-shaped aperture.

✶ Silver Set ✶

Three small crowns were cut from silver card (template on page 109) and two lines of holes pricked across the base of each one using a single-needle pricking tool (see Brilliant Baubles, pages 56–59). A clear gemstone was attached to the centre of each crown and they were then mounted onto an orange single-fold card using adhesive foam pads. Small quilled coils for the crown points were made from 10cm (4in) lengths of red 3mm (⅛in) wide paper strip.

✶ Crowning Glory ✶

An aperture was cut in a purple single-fold card using the largest crown template on page 109. A piece of red card was attached to the back panel of the card, on which was mounted a gold and smaller purple crown. The aperture and purple crown were then edged with gold pen. Three quilled coils for the crown points were formed from gold-edged red paper strip, the central coil made larger by allowing the coil to release slightly more.

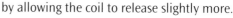

There Came Three Kings

* *

You will need

* red card in one paler and one darker shade 10cm (4in) square
* 3mm (⅛in) wide copper-edged pale red paper strip
* gold single-fold card 15 x 10.5cm (6 x 4⅛in)
* gold pen
* quilling tool
* Basic Tool Kit (see page 8)

*A wealth
of warm wishes
for you at
Christmas*

* quick & clever *

This would make
an ideal wedding card
for a couple getting
married over the
festive season.

step one Photocopy the two large crown templates and heart template on page 109 onto paper and cut out, then draw around the larger crown and heart onto the paler shade of red card, and around the smaller crown onto the darker shade of red card with a sharp HB pencil. Cut out with a medium-sized pair of scissors. (If making more than one card, draw around onto scrap card and cut out to make your own templates.)

step two Using PVA (white) glue, stick the two crowns together, then stick the heart in the centre. Draw two slightly arched lines across the bottom of the smaller, darker red crown with gold pen. If you don't feel confident drawing these freehand, draw lightly in pencil first. Draw around the heart with the pen to outline it.

* *

step three
Cut three 40cm (15¾in) lengths of the red paper strip. Holding the quilling tool in one hand, insert one end of one paper strip through the prongs of the quilling tool. Feed about 3mm (⅛in) through the prongs, then start rotating the tool.

step four
Continue to rotate the quilling tool in one hand while maintaining tension on the paper strip with the other hand.

step five
When you reach the end of the strip, carefully remove the quilling tool. Let the coil release very slightly, then use a cocktail stick to place a dot of PVA (white) glue on the end of the strip and press to the coil. Repeat with the other paper strips.

quick & clever ✳

To help make coils of the same size, you can use a plastic template board with circles of differing sizes cut into it, specially designed for quilling, against which you can match your coils to one selected size.

step six
Attach the crown to the gold single-fold card using adhesive foam pads, placing the foam pads in the centre of the crown so that their white edges don't show. Using a cocktail stick, apply a thick layer of PVA (white) glue to the non-shiny, underside of the coils and attach one to the top of each crown point.

Tag it!

For this crown-themed tag, a crown shape was drawn onto gold card, then a second drawn alongside and adjoining it. The two crowns were then cut out as a single piece, scored down the centre and folded in half. A smaller purple crown was attached to the gold card and a gold rub-on star placed in the centre. Two lines were drawn below in gold pen. Three quilled coils were then made from silver-edged red paper strip and one glued to each crown point.

Christmas greetings from lands afar

Countdown to Christmas

This colourful, interactive advent card employs all the techniques demonstrated in the previous chapters, such as punches, tags and peel-off stickers. It is also ideal for using up those leftover pieces of card and decorative materials from other projects.

Six punched tags with number peel-off stickers are attached with brads and embroidery thread for the main card, and the reverse side of each tag decorated with a variety of images, the final '25' tag turning over to reveal a stack of gifts. The variations show how die-cut shapes as well as ready-made tags can create equally impactful designs.

✶ Stocking-Up for Christmas ✶

In this alternative countdown design, Christmas stocking shapes were die-cut from a variety of bright card colours, and the tops, toes and heels trimmed with coordinating gingham paper. The stockings were decorated with silver number peel-off stickers and mounted onto an orange single-fold card using adhesive foam pads. Large white peel-off number stickers for 20 and 25 were then applied to opposite corners of the front panel of the card.

✶ Jewel in the Crown ✶

Traditionally shaped, different-coloured ready-made tags were attached to a tall bright blue single-fold card with snowflake-shaped brads. Each tag was then decorated with a black peel-off number sticker. The crown was made in the same way as that featured in There Came Three Kings (pages 92–95), with quilled coils of bronze-edged red paper strip attached to the crown points, and mounted onto the card with adhesive foam pads.

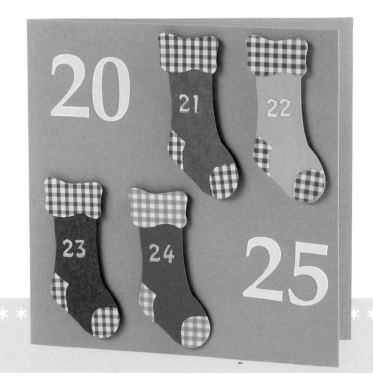

Countdown to Christmas

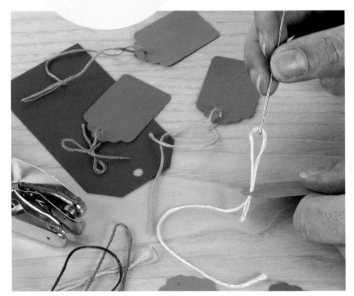

You will need

* red, blue, pink, orange, purple, green, turquoise scraps of card
* green single-fold card 15cm (6in) square
* green card 14.5cm (5¾in) square
* embroidery needle and embroidery thread in various colours
* silver number peel-off stickers 2cm (¾in) high
* blue number peel-off stickers 3cm (1⅛in) high
* large pre-cut red tag
* 7 decorative peel-off stickers or other embellishments
* 7 brads in different bright colours
* tag punch
* mini holepunch
* glass-headed pin
* Basic Tool Kit (see page 8)

✳ quick & clever ✳

To save time, you can use ready-cut tags purchased from a stationery store or suppliers.

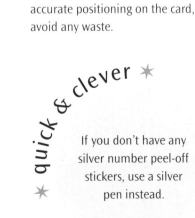

step one Punch a tag from each of the colours of scrap card. Here, the punch is held upside down to allow accurate positioning on the card, to avoid any waste.

step two

Using a mini holepunch, make a hole in the top of each tag. Thread an embroidery needle with a 12cm (4¾in) length of embroidery thread. Take the thread through the hole made in one contrasting-coloured tag. Tie the thread in a bow and trim the excess. Repeat with the other tags.

✳ quick & clever ✳

If you don't have any silver number peel-off stickers, use a silver pen instead.

step three
Place one silver peel-off sticker of numbers 19 to 24 on each of the punched tags, using a craft knife to lift them from the sheet to allow for easier positioning. Place the larger blue 2 and 5 peel-off stickers on the pre-cut red tag.

step four Decorate the reverse of each tag with peel-off stickers or other embellishments. The following were used here: 19 glitter snowflake, 20 holly Magic Motif™, 21 snowman resin peel-off sticker, 22 punched silver tree, 23 stocking peel-off sticker, 24 silver crown peel-off sticker with stars, 25 stack of gifts embossed peel-off sticker.

Hoping all your Christmas wishes come true

step five Open out the green single-fold card and place on a cutting mat or foam pad. Position the large red tag in the centre and the six smaller tags either side. Using a glass-headed pin, prick seven holes in the green card where you want the brads to go.

step six Insert a brad into each hole, then open out the 'wings' and flatten on the reverse of the card. Loop a tag onto each brad on the front of the card.

Tag it!

For this Christmas countdown tag, large, green peel-off stickers of numbers 2 and 5 were attached to the centre of a deep red ready-made luggage tag. Silver peel-off stickers of the numbers of the previous days in December were then attached at random over the surrounding area of the tag. A length of gold ribbon was threaded through the tag hole and tied in a knot.

step seven Place double-sided adhesive tape along each edge of the green square of card, remove the backing tape and position the card on the reserve of the front panel of the single-fold card so that it covers all the brad 'wings'. This also makes the card safer if you are giving it to small children.

Super-Quick Gallery

This gallery of Christmas card designs is for those occasions when you have run perilously short of time, but just can't bring yourself to admit defeat and settle for a purchased ready-made card. Here, toppers, peel-off stickers and other instant embellishments are put to creative use to make super-speedy cards in a matter of minutes.

✳ Trinket Tree ✳

In this design, the wide selection of brads that gather on any card-maker's work surface are put to effective use. A tree shape has been formed by arranging sizes and colours on a plain white linen-textured card. The 'wings' of the brads were then covered on the reverse side with a piece of card (see step seven of Countdown to Christmas, page 99).

✳ Metallic Miniatures ✳

A stack of three charming metal plaques adorns this tall blue card. Before mounting them, a strip of tissue paper flecked with gold was attached down the centre of the front panel of the card. The self-adhesive plaques were then speedily positioned over the tissue paper.

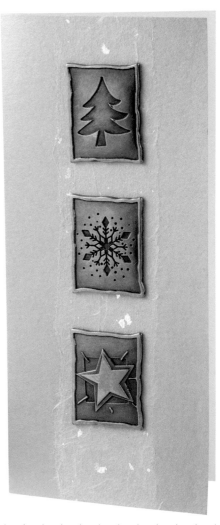

✳ Santa's Retreat ✳

With toppers, the main work is already
done for you, but there is still a need
to provide the right backdrop. Here, a
Santa's outfit, list and sack of gifts were
mounted onto a bright green card square,
then attached to a green single-fold card
using a tree-shaped brad in each corner.
A mini coat hanger and glasses convey a
sense of the absent man himself, no doubt
snatching a snooze!

✳ Gift Store ✳

Resin peel-off stickers are an absolute
essential in the last-minute card-maker's
emergency armoury. These different-
shaped stickers are carefully positioned to
fill a square of zingy orange card, which is
then mounted onto a pink square single-
fold card for an extra boost of vibrancy.

✳ Novel Noel ✳

For a classical look, a dark green single-fold
card was used to highlight elegant peel-off
letter stickers spelling 'Noel'. A length of gold
ribbon was wrapped around the upper portion
of the card, then a distinctive plaque-style
3-D peel-off sticker of a deer, again with the
word 'Noel', placed centrally over the top.

✳ Scrapbook Style ✳

This card is ideal to send to a relative to show how
the family is growing up. Two photos were placed
under metal slide mounts, which were then attached
to a red single-fold card using decorative brads. A
sticker string of Christmas lights was cut into three
lengths and placed above and between the photos,
with the ends wrapped around the edges of the card
and taped in place.

* Playful Pixies *

Who could resist these cheeky Christmas pixies! The row of four small resin peel-off stickers was mounted onto a strip of green card, which was then glued to a green single-fold card with the fold at the top. The larger pixie was mounted onto pale green card and then a larger rectangle of darker green card. This was placed at the end of the row using adhesive foam pads. White circles were punched using a regular office holepunch and glued over the background.

* Snow Screen *

A blue square single-fold card was covered all over with fine white tissue paper with fibres. A large die-cut snowflake was glued to the centre of the card, then embellished with dots of blue glitter glue. A snowflake-shaped brad was then inserted into each of the four corners of the card.

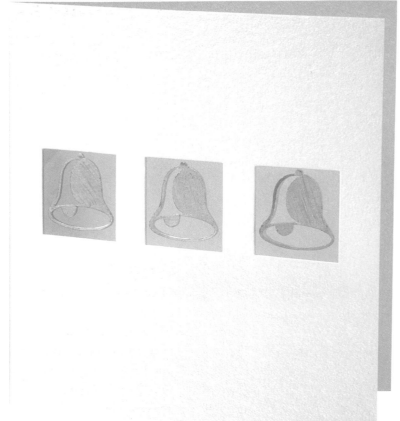

✳ Swaying Trees ✳

Tags are a brilliant way to make fast cards, and here a series of five were punched from pale green card. Tree-shaped resin peel-off stickers were placed on each tag and the tags attached to a long, narrow, deep pink single-fold card using metallic brads. A length of narrow green ribbon was then tied around the top of the card and tied in a bow to one side.

✳ Shimmering Bells ✳

A card with a row of three pre-cut apertures was used here, with a piece of acetate placed behind the apertures and secured with double-sided adhesive tape. The bell images are laser-cut shapes, which were coloured in using a gold pen and then glued to the centre of each aperture.

✶ Scenic Route ✶

Rainbow-coloured paper is the key to this atmospheric design. A black outline peel-off sticker of three camels was placed on the rainbow paper and then cut out. This was then glued to a landscape-shaped dark purple single-fold card. Gold star and diamond peel-off stickers were then added around the central panel, with a few sprinkled in the desert sky above the camels.

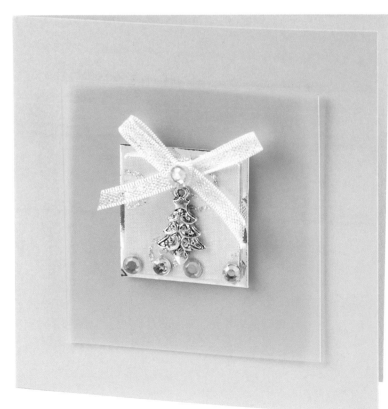

✶ Pleasing Pastels ✶

A soft pastel green colour scheme sets off this silver Christmas tree topper to best effect. The topper was first placed on a square of pale green-tinted plastic. This was then secured to the subtly coloured square single-fold card by only placing glue behind the topper so that it cannot be seen.

Templates

All templates are printed full size except those below. Enlarge these two templates on a photocopier at 200%, or the box can be enlarged to the size you require.

**Box
(page 17)
shown
at 50%**

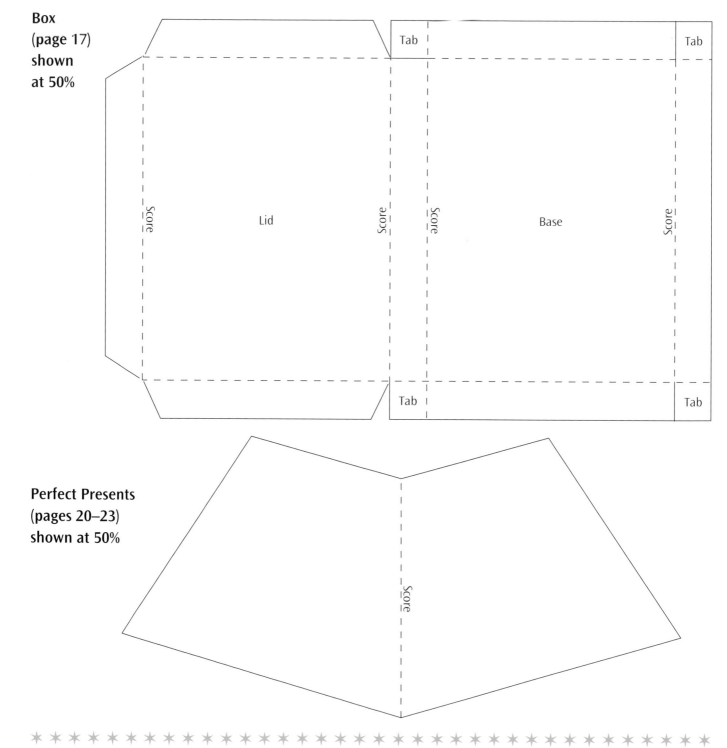

Tab

Tab

Score

Lid

Score

Score

Base

Score

Tab

Tab

**Perfect Presents
(pages 20–23)
shown at 50%**

Score

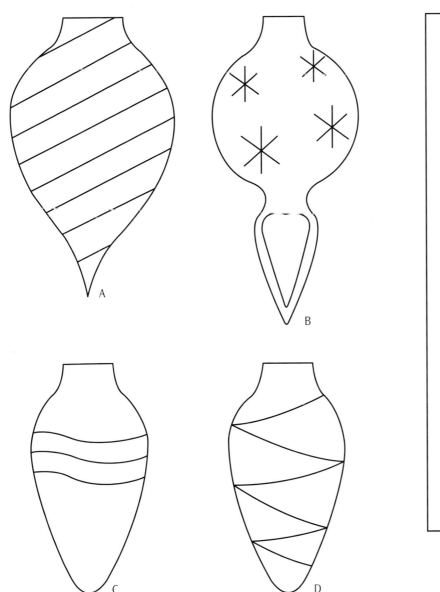

A

B

C

D

Brilliant Baubles (pages 56–59)

Winter Welcome (pages 60–63)

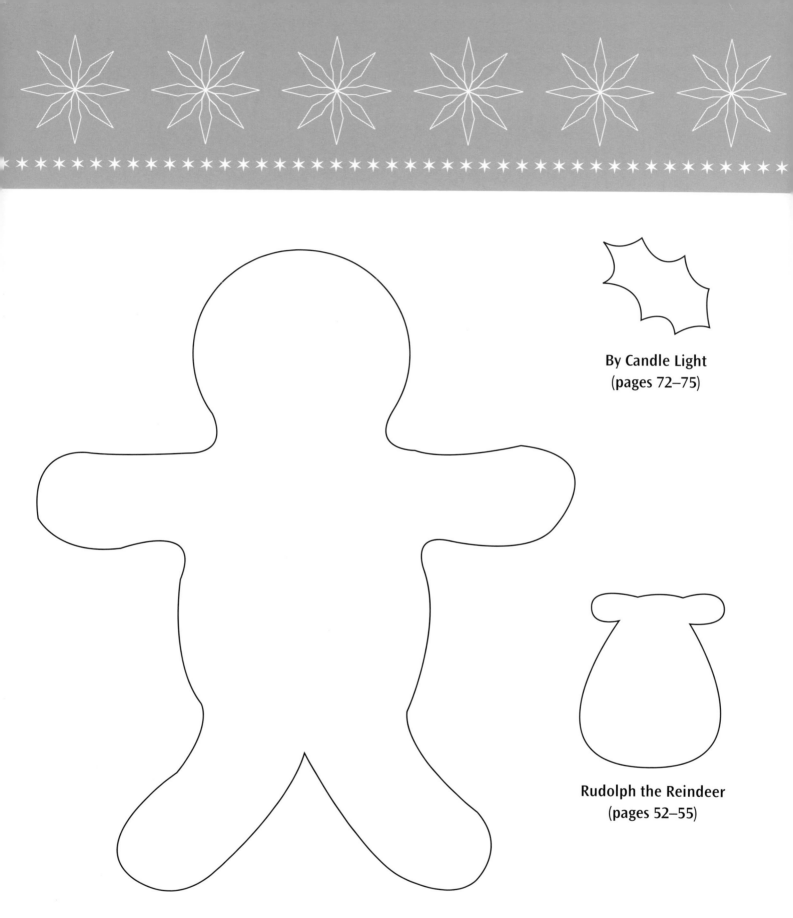

By Candle Light
(pages 72–75)

Rudolph the Reindeer
(pages 52–55)

Jolly Gingerbread Man (pages 24–27)

Sparkling Stars (pages 32–35)

There Came Three Kings (pages 92–95)

Silver Set (page 92)

Materials and Suppliers

Jolly Gingerbread Man
(pages 24–27)
Glaze pen: Sakura
White 3-D paint: Pebeo

Tag (page 27)
Resin peel-off sticker: Crystal Effects
Stickers Christmas A - DCCY30,
Dovecraft™

Home Sweet Home (page 24)
Gingerbread house topper:
Jolee's Boutique®
Rubber stamp: Gingerbread Wreath
SHO 200011, Card-io

Gingerbread Gang (page 24)
Wooden toppers: Habico

Simply Snow (pages 28–31)
Embossing system: Fiskars®
ShapeBoss™ and 'Winter Wonderland'
embossing stencil
Punch: Snowflake, The Punch Bunch

Winter Tapestry (page 28)
Corner brads: Queen & Co

Snow Drops (page 28)
Printed paper: 'Chelsea Pier',
Imagination Project

Starry Night (pages 36–39)
Rubber stamp: 'Catching the Stars'
2990K, Penny Black
Gold rub-on stars: E-Z Transfers,
Royal & Langnickel

Prickly Kisses (page 36)
Rubber stamp: 'Wishes for Kisses'
1505H, Penny Black

Baubling Along (page 36)
Rubber stamp: 'Merriest Xmas'
2529K, Penny Black

Pretty Poinsettias (pages 44–47)
Rubber stamp: Poinsettia 02.087N,
Woodware
Glaze pen: Sakura

Gorgeously Gilded (page 44)
Rubber stamp: Floral Holiday Trio
37.144N, Woodware

Flowery Gates (page 44)
Rubber stamp: Poinsettia Panel
29.104L, Woodware

Ring Out the Bells (pages 48–51)
Bells Magic Motifs™: Glue Dots™
International
Gold foil: Glue Dots™ International
White embossed card: Ivory
Christmas Trees, K&Co

Window Shopping (page 48)
Gifts Magic Motifs™. Glue Dots™
International
Gold rub-on stars: E-Z transfers,
Royal & Langnickel

Sparkling Sprig (page 48)
Holly Magic Motifs™: Glue Dots™
International

Rudolph the Reindeer
(pages 52–55)
Silver bells: Goldline® products,
from Tollit & Harvey
Gold bells: 6mm, Groves and Banks
Wire: Craft Creations

Tag (page 55)
Father Christmas topper: Habico
Bells: Gold Liberty Bells, Impex

Wrong-Footed Reindeer (page 52)
Reindeer punch: The Punch Bunch

Red-Nosed Reveller (page 52)
Silver bell: Goldline® products,
from Tollit & Harvey

Brilliant Baubles (pages 56–59)
Pricking tools: Pergamano®
Gold 3-D paint: Pebeo

Silver Strung (page 56)
Die-cut bauble: Ellison®

Winter Welcome
(pages 60–63)
Laser-cut wreaths: Rayher®
Hobby Gmbh

Spinning Angel (pages 64–67)
Rubber stamp: 'Silly Angel' E3119,
Hero Arts®
Dual-tipped marker pens: Letraset®
ProMarker pens – blush, pastel blue
Glaze pen: Sakura
Circle cutter and template: Fiskars®
ShapeTemplate™ and ShapeCutter™
Fibre thread: Make Me!, Kars

Santas Galore (pages 68–71)
Embossed peel-off sticker:
Christmas 551442, K&Co

Tag (page 71)
Embossed peel-off sticker: Christmas
551442, K&Co

Santa's Star Turn (page 68)
Embossed peel-off sticker: Christmas
Characters 552012, K&Co

Santa's Special Delivery (page 68)
Embossed peel-off sticker: Christmas
551442, K&Co

By Candle Light (pages 72–75)
Quilling papers: 1cm wide metallic,
Jane Jenkins Quilling Design

A Christmas Carol (page 72)
No-set eyelets: Hot Off The Press™

Flame Frame (page 72)
Die-cut holly leaves: Ellison®

Across the Miles (pages 76–79)
Acrylic paint: Pearl White, Gleaming
Sapphire Blue, Royal & Langnickel
Printed paper for scarf: Hot Off
The Press™
Glaze pens: Sakura

Tag (page 79)
Die-cut mittens: Ellison®

Winter Warmer (page 76)
Printed papers: Hot Off The Press™

Snow Pal (page 76)
Printed papers: Hot Off The Press™

Fantasy Greetings (pages 80–83)
Fibre: Fantasy Fiber™, Art Institute
Glitter Inc
Tag maker: Making Memories®
Christmas tree punch: The Punch Bunch

Hang Out the Stockings
(pages 84–87)
Die-cut stockings: Ellison®
Fun Flock: Craft Creations
Printed papers: Hot Off The Press™

All Lined Up (page 84)
Printed papers: Hot Off The Press™

Stocking Surprise (page 84)
Stocking toys: 'Whimsical Christmas'
Artsy Collage™ booklet, Hot Off
The Press™

Ice skating Fun (pages 88–91)
Peel-off stickers: XL031U black,
Craft Creations

There Came Three Kings
(pages 92–95)
Quilling papers: 3mm wide
metallic-edged red, Jane Jenkins
Quilling Design

Countdown to Christmas
(pages 96–99)
Tag punch: Woodware
Number peel-off stickers: 2cm ZL405U
silver, 3cm ZL407U blue,
Craft Creations

Super-Quick Gallery
Metallic Miniatures (page 100)
Metal plaques: 'Winter', Making
Memories®

Santa's Retreat (page 101)
Santa outfit: Santa's Suit SPJB042,
Jolee's Boutique®

Gift Store (page 101)
Resin peel-off stickers:
'Gifts, Spots and Stripes', PaperMania

Novel Noel (page 102)
Peel-off stickers: 'Holiday Traditions'
die-cut alphabet 553316; 'Holiday
Celebrations' 555150, K&Co

Scrapbook Style (page 102)
Metal slide mounts: 558113, K&Co
Sticker: Christmas lights, Jolee's Boutique®

Playful Pixies (page 103)
Resin peel-off stickers: Crystal
Effects Stickers Christmas C-DCCY32,
Dovecraft™

Snow Screen (page 103)
Die-cut snowflake: Craftwork Cards
Snowflake brads: PaperMania

Swaying Trees (page 104)
Resin peel-off stickers: Christmas tree
selection, PaperMania

Shimmering Bells (page 104)
Die-cut bells: Paper State

Scenic Route (page 105)
Peel-off sticker: XL591U black,
Craft Creations
Rainbow paper: HobbyCraft

Pleasing Pastels (page 105)
Topper: Tree Ribbon, Paper Cellar

Card-io
Unit 15–16
Swan Meadow Estate
Swan Meadow Road
Wigan WN3 5BJ
Tel: 01942 237238
www.card-io.com

Centagraph
18 Station Parade
Harrogate
North Yorkshire HG1 1UE
Tel: 01423 566327
www.centagraph.co.uk

Craft Creations Ltd
Ingersoll House
Delamare Road
Cheshunt
Hertfordshire EN8 9HD
Tel: 01992 781900
www.craftcreations.co.uk

Craftwork Cards Ltd
Unit 2
The Moorings
Waterside Road
Stourton
Leeds
West Yorkshire LS10 1RW
Tel: 0113 276 5713
www.craftworkcards.com

DoCrafts
Design Objectives Ltd
Unit 90
Woolsbridge Industrial Park
Three Legged Cross
Wimborne
Dorset BH15 6SU
Tel: 01202 811000
www.docrafts.co.uk

Dovecraft™
www.dovecraft.com

Efco
Sinotex UK Ltd
Unit D
The Courtyard Business Centre
Lonesome Lane
Reigate
Surrey RH2 7QT
Tel: 01737 245450
Email: info@artys.co.uk

Fiskars UK Ltd
Newlands Avenue
Brackland Industrial Estate
Bridgend
Mid Glamorgan CF31 2XA
Tel: 01656 655595
www.fiskars.com

Glue Dots™ International Ltd
Unit 1 Coronation Business Park
Hard Ings Road
Keighley
West Yorkshire BD21 3ND
Tel: 01535 616290
www.gluedotsuk.co.uk

Groves and Banks
Drakes Drive Industrial Estate
Long Crendon
Aylesbury HP18 9BA
Tel: 01844 258100
www.groves-banks.com

Habico Ltd
Tong Road Industrial Estate
Amberley Road
Leeds LS12 4BD
Tel: 0113 263 1500
www.habico.co.uk

HobbyCraft stores
Tel: 0800 027 2387 for nearest
store or mail order is available
www.hobbycraft.co.uk

Impex Creative Crafts Ltd
Impex House
Atlas Road
Wembley
Middlesex HA9 0TX
Tel: 020 8900 0999
www.impexcreativecrafts.co.uk

Jane Jenkins Quilling Design
33 Mill Rise
Skidby
Cottingham
East Yorkshire HU16 5UA
Tel: 01482 843721
www.jjquilling.co.uk

Lakeland Limited
Alexandra Buildings
Windermere
Cumbria LA23 1BQ
Tel: 015394 88100
www.lakelandlimited.com

Letraset® Limited
Kingsnorth Industrial Estate
Wotton Road
Ashford
Kent TN23 6FL
Tel: 01233 624421
www.letraset.com

Paper Cellar Ltd
Langley Place
99 Langley Road
Watford
Hertfordshire WD17 4AU
Tel: 0871 8713711
www.papercellar.com

PaperMania
www.papermania.co.uk
see DoCrafts

Pebeo UK Ltd
Solent Business Centre
Millbrook Road West
Millbrook
Southampton
Hampshire SO15 0HW
Tel: 02380 901914
www.pebeo.com

Personal Impressions
EM Richford Ltd
Curzon Road
Chilton Industrial Estate
Sudbury
Suffolk CO10 2XW
Tel: 01787 375241
www.richstamp.co.uk

The Stamp Bug Ltd
Unit 3
The Old Sawmill Workshops
Hatherop
Near Cirencester
Gloucester GL7 3NA
Tel: 01285 750308
www.thestampbug.co.uk

Tollit & Harvey Ltd
Oldmeadow Road
Kings Lynn
Norfolk PE30 4LW
Tel: 01553 696600
www.tollitandharvey.co.uk

Woodware Craft Collection Ltd
Unit 2a
Sandylands Business Park
Skipton
North Yorkshire BD23 2DE
Tel: 01756 700024
Email: sales@woodware.co.uk

XCut®
www.xcuttools.com
see DoCrafts

Karen Marie Klip®
Bomhusvej 3
6300 Gråsten
Denmark
Tel: +45 74 65 22 56
www.karenmarieklip.dk

Kars Creative Wholesale
Industrieweg 27
Industrieterrein "De Heuning"
Postbus 97
4050 EB Ochten
The Netherlands
Tel: +31(0) 344 642864
www.kars.nl

Pergamano®
Pergamano International
P O Box 86
1420 AB Uithoorn
The Netherlands
Tel: +31(0) 297 522 533
www.pergamano.com

Rayher® Hobby GmbH
D-88471 Laupheim
Germany
Tel: 07392/7005-0
www.rayher-hobby.de

Starform
Email: info@starform.nl
Fax: +31(0) 23 5570778
www.starform.nl

Art Institute Glitter Inc
712 N Balboa Street
Cottonwood, Arizona 86326
Tel: 877 909 0805
www.artglitter.com

Ellison® Educational Equipment Inc
25862 Commercentre Drive
Lake Forest
California 92630-8804
Tel: 800 253 2238
www.ellison.com

Hero Arts®
1343 Powell Street
Emeryville
California 94608
Tel: 800 822 HERO
www.heroarts.com

Hot Off The Press™ Inc
1250 NW Third
Canby OR 97013
Tel: 888 300 3406
www.paperwishes.com

Imagination Project
9465 Sutton Place
Hamilton, Ohio 45011
Tel: 888 477 6532
www.imaginationproject.com

Jolee's Boutique® at Stickopotamus®
P O Box 1047
Clifton, NJ 07014-1047
www.stickopotamus.com

K&Co
11125 N.W. Ambassador Drive
Suite 200
Kansas City MO 64153
Tel: 888 244 2083
www.kandcompany.com

Making Memories®
1168 West 500 North
Centerville, Utah 84014
Tel: 801 294 0430
www.makingmemories.com

Michaels' Stores
8000 Bent Branch Dr
Irving, TX 75063
Tel: 1 800 642 4235
www.michaels.com

Penny Black Inc
P O Box 11496
Berkeley, CA 94712
www.penyblackinc.com

Plaid Enterprises Inc
P O Box 7600
Norcross, GA 30091-7600
Tel: 800 842 4197
www.plaidonline.com

The Punch Bunch
2819 W Adams Ave
Temple, TX 76504
Tel: 254 791 4209
www.thepunchbunch.com

Queen & Co
P O Box 501773
San Diego, CA 92150
Tel: 858 613 7858
www.queenandcompany.com

Royal & Langnickel
Royal Brush Mfg
6707 Broadway
Merrillville, IN 46410
Tel: 800 247 2211
www.royalbrush.com

Rubber Stamp Tapestry
326 Adams Road
Seagrove, NC 27341
Tel: 336 879 6650
www.rubberstamptapestry.com

Sakura of America
30780 San Clemente Street
Hayward, CA 94544
www.gellyroll.com

Sugarloaf Products Inc
see www.sugarloafproducts.com for retailers of Whispers™ and Anita's Art Stamps and Anita's Art peel-off stickers

Tsukineko, Inc
17640 NE 65th Street
Redmond, WA 98052
Tel: 425 883 7733
www.tsukineko.com
For stockists of VersaMark™ and StazOn™

✳ About the Author ✳

Elizabeth Moad is a successful card maker, workshop tutor and author, regularly contributing to craft magazines, such as *Crafts Beautiful*, *Quick & Crafty!* and *Let's Make Cards!* Her passion for art and crafts led her to undertake further study in order to pursue a creative career. This is her third book published by David & Charles. Elizabeth lives in Ipswich, East Anglia, in the UK. For more information, see www.elizabethmoad.com.

✳ Acknowledgments ✳

Many thanks to Cheryl Brown, Bethany Dymond, Jenny Fox-Proverbs, Pru Rogers and Tracey Woodward at David & Charles. Special thanks to Jo Richardson, Karl Adamson, Selina Jackson and my family and friends for all their support.

Index